ONE HUNDRED EIGHTY LANDINGS OF UNITED STATES MARINES
1800-1934

By Captain Harry Allanson Ellsworth, USMC

HISTORY AND MUSEUMS DIVISION
HEADQUARTERS, U. S. MARINE CORPS
WASHINGTON, D. C.
1974

For sale by the Superintendent of Documents, U.S. Government Printing Office
Washington, D.C. 20402 - Price $3.00
Stock Number 008-055-00078-5

Cover: Men of the Marine Corps Expeditionary Force landing at Culebra, Puerto Rico during fleet maneuvers, winter of 1923-24. (USMC Photo 515096)

DEPARTMENT OF THE NAVY
HEADQUARTERS UNITED STATES MARINE CORPS
WASHINGTON, D.C. 20380

FOREWORD

In 1934, Captain Harry Alanson Ellsworth, USMC, who served as Officer-in-Charge of the Historical Section, Adjutant & Inspectors Department, Headquarters, U. S. Marine Corps, produced a mimeographed booklet entitled One Hundred Eighty Landings of United States Marines 1800-1934. This work was reprinted in 1964, and a continued demand for the compilation has led to this second reprint.

The Ellsworth history has been published in exact facsimile. No attempt has been made to validate or edit it. Mr. Ralph W. Donnelly of the Reference Section of the History and Museums Division has provided a preface which expands on the subject of international landings by Marines and provides biographical data on Captain Ellsworth.

The basic material of the pamphlet is sound and the listed sources will give readers a starting point for further research. The History and Museums Division invites constructive comments on the content.

E. H. SIMMONS
Brigadier General, U. S. Marine Corps (Ret.)
Director of Marine Corps History and Museums

Reviewed and approved:
29 October 1974

PREFACE

Ellsworth's _180 Landings_, to use its popular title, has not been superseded by a more detailed or comprehensive coverage since its original publication forty years ago. The most comparable listing is to be found in _Background Information on the Use of United States Armed Forces in Foreign Countries_, a print of the Subcommittee on National Security Policy and Scientific Developments of the Committee on Foreign Affairs. This is a committee print from the 2d Session, 91st Congress made in 1970 as an up-date of a 1951 publication of the same title. The eight pages of Appendix II (pages 50-57) are a chronological listing of the use of U. S. Armed Forces abroad from 1798 to 1970.

Ellsworth's _180 Landings_ concerns itself with four basic causes for landings: (1) political intervention, (2) punitive actions, (3) protection of diplomatic mission, nationals, and their property, and (4) humanitarian. Many of these landings were solely Marine Corps affairs, a number were joint with Navy personnel. International cooperation with one or more foreign powers characterize some of these.

The effect of landing Marines on international law has long been a matter of legal speculation. The virtual abandonment of the Monroe Doctrine, the dropping of the Platt Amendment, the elimination of the "Open Door" policy in China, and the development of international organizations such as the Organization of American States and the United Nations have created a new climate in international relations.

As a result, political interventions and punitive actions no longer occur as frequently as in the Corps' early days. Landings for humanitarian reasons are still carried out and are non-controversial in the international community. Landings for the protection of diplomatic missions are no longer "landings," but have assumed a permanence hitherto not achieved by Marines assigned to this duty. The establishment of Legation guards at Tokyo in 1868, at Seoul in 1888, at Peking in 1900, and at Managua in 1913 finally led to the regular assignment of Marine guards attached to diplomatic and consular establishments as security guards beginning with a Memorandum Agreement with the Department of State signed on 15 December 1948.

This program has expanded until today (1 July 1974) there are 114 Security Guards stationed throughout the world calling on the services of about 1,100 Marines and with an expected expansion to 1,500 Marines.

Within the Marine Corps there has been a long history of a legend that the landing of Marines on foreign soil was not considered as an act of war while on the other hand the landing of Army troops would in all probability be considered as an overt act of war, and result in such.

Such an exception is not to be found in international law, and, as a matter of fact, a number of other countries have used soldiers under the same right for taking such action as we claim for the use of Marines. The almost exclusive use of Marines for landings in foreign countries by the United States may be ascribed to force of habit and a history of dependable and speedy reaction time in contrast to the greater deliberation by the Army when called upon for similar service.

The legal basis for the landing of troops in foreign countries both for intervention and interposition has been explored at length in a State Department pamphlet, <u>Right to Protect Citizens in Foreign Countries by Landing Forces</u>. The Third Revised Edition was printed in 1934.

The basic principles developed in this study were:

(1) The Marines have no special authority, nor any special privilege, by which armed forces might be ordered to land on foreign territory.

(2) By reason of the special character of Marine training and service afloat, in all parts of the world, Marines have in most cases been most readily at hand for armed intervention and/or interposition.

(3) In the opinion of experts in the Department of State, the President does have constitutional authority in some cases---difficult of definition---to order Marines or other armed forces ashore in foreign territory without reference to Congress, which alone can declare war.

Harry Alanson Ellsworth, the author-compiler of this work, was born 9 March 1883 at Prattsburg, N. Y. His first military experience was an enlistment in the U. S. Army covering 2 October 1899 until 27 June 1901. He then served four enlistments in the Marine Corps beginning 18 November 1903 and terminating 28 March 1917, with a seven months break between his first and second enlistment.

During 1911, Ellsworth, then a corporal, worked with Corporal Charles D. Baylis and retired Sergeant Major Edward Dunn in organizing and processing the old records books of the Marine Corps.

He was appointed a quartermaster clerk in March 1917 and was assigned to duty briefly at Headquarters Marine Corps. Receiving a commission as a second lieutenant in July, Ellsworth was assigned to the 7th Regiment and served with this unit in Cuba during World War I. Returning to the United States with the temporary rank of captain, he soon returned to Headquarters where he remained until the fall of 1922.

He reported to Marine Barracks, Quantico, on 2 October 1922, where he attended and graduated from the Company Officers' Course. This was followed by three years with the 1st Marine Brigade in Haiti. Between November 1925 and July 1930 Ellsworth was at the Naval Ammunition Depot, Hingham, Mass.; Marine Barracks, Quantico; and Marine Barracks, Parris Island, S. C.

In July 1930 he again served with the 1st Brigade in Haiti, returning to Headquarters in February 1933. Between 3 March 1933 and 30 August 1934, Ellsworth was Officer-in-Charge of the Historical Section. He then served at the Navy Yard, Washington, D. C., until his retirement with the rank of major on 30 June 1939 after 36 years, 9 months, and 12 days service.

The Marine Corps build-up prior to World War II resulted in Ellsworth being recalled for active duty on 1 June 1940 at Marine Barracks, Pensacola Naval Air Station, where he served until he was returned to retired status as of 20 December 1942.

Major Ellsworth died 19 June 1962 at the U. S. Naval Hospital on the U. S. S. Haven at Long Beach, California, in his 80th year.

Ellsworth devised a filing system which he named the "Ells-Dran Filing System." The "Ells" are the first four letters of his surname, and the "Dran" are the first letters of the words "Direct-Reference-Alphabetical-Numerical," descriptive word-titles of the major points of the system. The system was adopted by the Marine Corps in 1935 and used until 30 June 1950 for Headquarters files.

One article, a "Calendar of Important Events in the History of United States Marines 1775-1935," was prepared by Ellsworth and published in the Marine Corps Gazette for November 1935.

ONE HUNDRED EIGHTY LANDINGS OF UNITED STATES MARINES

1800 - 1934

A BRIEF HISTORY IN TWO PARTS

PART ONE

By

CAPTAIN HARRY ALANSON ELLSWORTH, U. S. MARINE CORPS

OFFICER IN CHARGE, HISTORICAL SECTION

FIRST EDITION

1934

(ABYSSINIA to FEEJEE ISLANDS)

FOREWORD

Much has been written about the activities of the United States Marines in actual warfare -- the highly creditable part they have played, and the efficiency with which that part of their mission has been performed. But there is still another part of their mission -- perhaps the most important -- which barely has been touched upon by any writer other than in a headline of the daily newspapers to the effect that, "THE MARINES HAVE LANDED, AND HAVE THE SITUATION WELL IN HAND." Little does the average American citizen realize what that oft repeated statement portends, and its real significance in relation to the protection of nationals of the United States residing in foreign lands. The guarding of these interests, together with the rendering of able assistance to their Country's diplomatic representatives in establishing and maintaining foreign policies, have long been their most important duty.

"From the Halls of Montezuma to the Shores of Tripoli" tells not half the story. In every quarter of the Globe, under every conceivable adverse condition, the United States Marines have fought side by side with the Navy and at times with the Army, foreign soldiers, marines and sailors, but more often alone, protecting American lives and interests -- and that, without causing international complications.

Time after time they have been called upon to quell revolutions, whether in an incipient or advanced stage, to secure redress for crimes committed upon United States citizens, to resent insults to the flag, to render assistance in times of great disaster, and even to put down mutinies aboard foreign men-of-war at the earnest solicitation of the vessel's commander. No matter what the task might be, the Marines have ever emerged with flying colors, worthy of the highest commendation.

These angles of the Marines' well rounded mission and their relations with foreign countries in time of peace thus far have not been compiled. In the pages that follow the author has undertaken to set forth an accurate account of the Landings in foreign lands. The information upon which this history is based has been secured from official records exclusively, and the useless expatiation of unnecessary details, which might tend to obscure or cloud the facts, have been avoided.

To the memory of those Marines who have glorified their motto -- SEMPER FIDELIS -- this work is dedicated.

August 31st, 1934

CHRONOLOGY

		Page
1800	Dominican Republic	65
1804	Tripoli	157
1805	Tripoli	158
1813	Marquesas Islands	112
1814	Marquesas Islands	112
1824	Porto Rico	139
1831	Falkland Islands	76
1832	Falkland Islands	76
	Sumatra	151
1833	Argentina	9
1835	Peru	137
1836	Peru	138
1838	Sumatra	153
1839	Sumatra	154
1840	Feejee Islands	77
1841	Drummonds Island	72
	Samoa	144
1843	Africa	3
1851	Johanna Island	106
1852	Argentina	10
	Nicaragua	120
1853	Japan	99
	Luchu Islands	108
	Nicaragua	120
	Siam	150
1854	China	21
	Japan	100
	Luchu Islands	109
	Nicaragua	121
1855	China	23
	Feejee Islands	80
	Uruguay	160
1856	China	24
1858	Feejee Islands	81
	Uruguay	161
1859	China	27
1860	Africa	7
	Colombia	46
	Japan	102
1863	Japan	102
1866	China	28
1867	Formosa	83
	Japan	103
1868	Japan	103
	Uruguay	161
1870	Hawaiian Islands	92
	Mexico	114

(Chronology Continued)

		Page
1871	Corea	57
1873	Colombia	46
1874	Hawaiian Islands	92
1878	France	85
1882	Egypt	75
1885	Colombia	48
1888	Corea	59
	Haiti	88
	Samoa	146
1889	France	85
	Hawaiian Islands	92
1890	Argentina	13
	Japan	104
1891	Bering Sea (Seal Poaching)	14
	Chile	16
	Navassa Island	119
1893	Hawaiian Islands	93
1894	China	30
	Corea	59
	Nicaragua	122
1895	China	31
	Colombia	51
	Corea	60
	Trinidad (B.W.I.)	156
1896	Corea	60
	Nicaragua	122
1898	China	32
	Nicaragua	123
1899	China	33
	Nicaragua	123
	Samoa	146
1900	China	33
1901	Colombia	52
1902	Colombia	54
1903	Abyssinia	1
	Dominican Republic	66
	Honduras	94
	Panama	134
	Syria	155
1904	Africa	8
	Corea	60
	Dominican Republic	66
	Panama	138
1905	China	39
	Corea	60
	France	86
	Russia	141
1906	Cuba	62
1907	Honduras	95

(Chronology Continued)

		Page
1910	Nicaragua	124
1911	China	40
1912	China	40
	Cuba	62
	Nicaragua	125
1913	China	41
	Mexico	115
1914	Haiti	88
	Mexico	116
1915	Haiti	89
1916	Dominican Republic	69
1917	Cuba	63
1918	Russia	141
1919	Russia	142
1920	Russia	143
1922	China	41
	Nicaragua	128
1924	China	42
	Honduras	96
1925	China	42
	Honduras	98
	Nicaragua	128
1926	China	42
	Nicaragua	129
1927-34	China	43
1927	Nicaragua	131
1928-33	Nicaragua	133
1934	Russia	143

ABYSSINIA

(1903)

The United States Government was desirous of concluding a treaty of amity, reciprocity, and commerce with Emperor Menelik II. of Abyssinia. Accordingly, in the latter part of this year, the American Consul-General at Versailles, (Mr. Skinner), was instructed to proceed to Addis Ababa, Menelik's Capital, to arrange such a treaty.

Due to the long distance which had to be traversed in order to reach Menelik's domain, the fact that a greater part of the journey had to be made over desert and mountain, with only mules and camels for transportation, and that the way would be infested with half-savage tribes of natives, it was necessary that an escort be provided for the safety of the expedition.

The flagship *Brooklyn*, the *San Francisco* and *Machias* were in that vicinity, and they were called upon to furnish Marines for this escort. Captain George C. Thorpe, of the Marines, 19 enlisted Marines and 6 sailors were detailed from the *Brooklyn* and *San Francisco*. They took passage on the *Machias* to Djibouti, French Somaliland, and reported to Lieutenant C. L. Hussey, of the Navy, (who was to command the expedition), on November 18, 1903. From Djibouti to Dire Daoua the trip was made by train, and the expedition arrived the evening of the 21st. It was now necessary to obtain the necessary mules and camels for the long trek of over three hundred miles to Addis Ababa. After surmounting many obstacles, the necessary animals were arranged for; equipage secured, camel drivers hired and the cavalcade consisting of 46 camels and 45 mules, got underway and proceeded on its journey.

Soon after the second day's movement started, Captain Thorpe experienced his first difficulty. This was with the Haban (chief camel man), over the route the caravan should take. There were three different trails, and Captain Thorpe desired to take the middle one, but the Haban insisted on the one to the right. It was only after binding him, hand and foot, that Captain Thorpe was enabled to convince him of his wayward tendencies and persuade him to take the route

(Abyssinia) 2

desired. The remainder of the journey was made without further trouble, except for an incident at one camp in Dankaliland. At this camp the King of one of the tribes visited the caravan and demanded 100 talers (about $47.00). He was refused, of course, and he then threatened an attack, which did not materialize.

On December 18th the caravan arrived to within about one hour's march from Addis Ababa, where they were met by a Frenchman acting as one of the Emperor's counsellors. Here they shifted into "special full dress uniforms," and in the afternoon started into the capital. The hills and plains were covered with thousands of the Emperor's warriors, fantastically dressed in lion or leopard skins, waiting to receive the Americans. The warriors were all well mounted on splendid Arabian horses or Zebra-like mules and, amidst great confusion, the din of trumpets and tom-toms, escorted the American Expedition to the Gebi, Menelik's palace. Here the Americans dismounted, entered the Gebi, and held their first conference with the Emperor.

During their ten day's stay at Addis Ababa the Americans were furnished with a "palace" and large compound for their camp, which proved in every way adequate to their needs, and very comfortable. On December 24th, the Emperor paid a visit to this camp, and Captain Thorpe had his men perform a few drills for the distinguished visitor, which pleased him greatly.

The work of the American Commissioner having been successfully completed, the little caravan was ready to start its return journey, but before they said their last farewells, the Emperor presented all the enlisted men with the Menelik medal and the Star of Ethiopia to Lieutenant Hussey and Captain Thorpe.

The return "voyage" was commenced on the 26th, and completed without notable incident – the caravan arriving at Djibouti on January 15, 1904. During the two months in Abyssinia, the little expedition made more than forty camps, and hoisted the American flag where it had never been seen before.

Reference: MC Archives – Original Report of Captain Thorpe.

AFRICA
(1843)

Piracy along the African Coast had assumed such proportions by the middle of this year, that the United States government decided to resort to the use of armed forces to rid these waters of these scourges of the sea. And piracy, alone, was not the only nefarious activity practiced on this coast. The slave trade being carried on was equally distasteful to the sensibilities of the American people, and it was decided to put an end to both of these unlawful practices by despatching a squadron of naval vessels to the scene, with instructions to use force if necessary to eliminate them.

The natives of the Sinoe and Berribee tribes were the principal offenders, and outstanding among the piratical crimes committed by them may be mentioned the case of the American vessels Mary Carver and Edward Barley. The Captain of the former had suffered unspeakable horrors at their hands, being bound and delivered to the tender mercies of the savage women and children who, past masters in the art of torture, contented themselves by sticking thorns in his flesh, as well as other forms of torture. In the case of the latter vessel, the captain, mate and cook had been cruelly murdered.

The American government deemed it necessary that an imposing force be employed in carrying out the mission of exacting redress for these crimes, as well as eliminating further piratical and slave trading activities in this area. Commodore Matthew C. Perry was not then on a cruise, so he and his squadron of four ships were selected for this exacting duty. The squadron consisted of the Decatur, Macedonian, Porpoise and Saratoga. Each of these vessels carried a Marine Guard, with the exception of the Porpoise. Two Marine officers - First Lieutenant Jabez C. Rich and Second Lieutenant Isaac T. Doughty were attached to the squadron, and stationed on the Macedonian and Saratoga respectively. Perry raised his broad pennant over the Saratoga on June 6th, at New York, and soon afterward sailed for the African coast. Sometime after leaving New York, his pennant was transferred to the Macedonian.

(Africa) 4

The squadron arrived off the African coast about midsummer, and around the first part of October, the Commodore decided to obtain first hand information relative to piratical activities of the natives. Accordingly, he disguised the *Porpoise* as a merchantman, concealed the Marines and sailors below the hatches, and sent her in towards shore off Berribee. The apparently harmless vessel had no more than anchored before the native canoes rushed out to capture her. As only a sample of their thieving proclivities was needed, Commander Stellwagen, satisfied with a good joke, refrained from opening fire on the native boats. This incident satisfied the Commodore, and he proceeded with his original mission.

Sinoe was selected as the starting place, and the squadron, less the *Porpoise* (which had been despatched on other duty), came to anchor off this place on November 27th and 28th -- the *Saratoga* preceding the flagship and the *Decatur* into the anchorage. Early in the morning of the 29th, Commodore Perry armed several boats with 75 Marines and sailors, and the procession moved to the Methodist Church, in which the palaver was to be held. Before the President of Liberia, Mr. Roberts, and the Commodore, with their respective staffs on the one side, and twenty "kings" or head men on the other, the murder of members of the crew of the *Edward Barley* was discussed. It appeared that the white man was the first aggressor, and the Fishmen and not the Sinoes were the culprits. After listening patiently to the black orators, Perry ordered the Fishmen's town to be burned, keeping three of them as hostages to be sent to Monrovia, and Perry and his party returned to the ship.

On December 1st, Perry, with Marines and sailors from the three vessels, again landed and proceeded to the town of Blue Barra to hold a palaver with the chiefs, and carry them presents, as an indication of the American's friendship. Having completed this mission the landing force returned in the afternoon. Shortly after midnight of the 3rd, the squadron got underway, sailed for Setra Kroo, and arrived there early in the afternoon. On the morning of the 5th, the Commodore again made a landing, with the Marines and sailors, for a palaver with the principal chief. This lasted until late in the afternoon when, apparently satisfied with his negotiations, Perry and the armed party

(Africa)

returned to their ships. His mission having been completed at this place, he sailed for Cape Palmas the same evening, and arrived there in the afternoon of the 7th, anchoring off the town of Caval.

The following morning, the 8th, Commodore Perry, with the Marines and sailors, made a landing for a conference with the King. The primary subject discussed at this conference was the removal of the capital to a place farther inland. However, no decision was reached, and another meeting was arranged for the following day at the royal kraal. About ten o'clock the next morning 10 armed boats from the three ships, loaded with Marines and sailors, accompanied the Commodore ashore for his palaver. When the boats arrived at the landing place they were met by about 50 natives who acted as an escort for Perry and his party to the village where the meeting was to take place.

The capital was a palisaded village, in the center of which was the palaver house. Most of the male warriors were conspicuous by their absence, while the women and children were hidden in the woods some distance away. King Crack-O did not put in an immediate appearance, and Perry, not to be surprised by any overt act on the part of the natives, ordered that Marine sentinels be posted at all gates. Finally "His Majesty" appeared, and the palaver began. Governor Roberts opened the conversations by referring to the murder of Captain Carver, of the schooner Mary Carver, and stated that the towns along the shore governed by King Crack-O were implicated in the crime. The King made a defiant denial to this charge, and to indicate his truthfulness in the statement, touched his ears and tongue symbolically to his sword. He was then questioned relative to his willingness to attend the "Great Palaver" at Little Berribee, to which he readily assented, and the meeting adjourned.

As there was nothing further to be gained by remaining longer at Caval, the squadron set sail on the 11th for Little Berribee (Half Bereby), where they arrived the next day. On December 14th, Commodore Perry selected some 200 Marines and sailors, embarked them in boats, and despatched

(Africa)

them shoreward. He followed them immediately, and when the whole party had landed, the march was begun to the village. The place selected for the meeting was about 50 yards from the town gate, inside of the palisades. King Ben Crack-O was present, and when the Commodore arrived, laid aside his long iron spear, and the palaver began. This had hardly started before it was manifest that "His Majesty" was a voluminous but skillful liar, and, himself, one of the most guilty of the thieves. His tergiversations soon became impudent and manifest, and his lies seemed to fall with a thump.

Governor Roberts issued repeated warnings to the King relative to his apparent untruths but these had little or no effect, and the Commodore, losing patience, stepped toward the offender and warned him to lie no more. Simultaneously, the native interpreter bolted from the house and fled to the woods, while at the same time King Crack-O moved closer toward Perry. Perry had sensed this act of treachery and was fully prepared when Crack-O seized him and tried to drag him to the place where the spear had been left, with the intention, no doubt, of using it to despatch the Commodore. The King found, however, that Perry was not to be so easily disposed of, for no sooner had he been seized by the burly black ruler than Perry threw him away from the direction of the stacked arms, whereupon the King commenced a retreat from the house, and no sooner had he passed through the door than he was shot by a sergeant of Marines, while other Marines inflicted upon his person two bayonet wounds, and he was finally bound and carried to the beach.

This incident ended the palaver, and it was the signal for a general melee in which irregular firing commenced from both sides, in spite of the Commodore's orders to refrain from so doing. This manifestation of hostilities induced the American commander to destroy the town. The torch was applied, and in about an hour it was a level waste. As the Americans were returning to their boats, the natives opened fire from the woods. This fire was returned by the Marines and sailors, and even the ships joined in the general attack to drive the natives beyond effective range of their rifles, and permit the landing party to gain their boats in safety.

(Africa)

King Ben Crack-O's spear was retained by Commodore Perry as a relic and trophy of his experiences along the coast of the "Dark Continent." An American flag was found in the palaver house, as well as pieces of the schooner *Mary Carver*, and these together with several war canoes were carried away to the ships as additional trophies in commemoration of a test at arms with the natives. King Crack-O died the following day aboard one of Perry's ships, and his body was committed to the deep.

The following day, the 16th, the squadron proceeded along the coast, and when a short distance from Little Berribee, another settlement was discovered. Perry signaled "all hands come to anchor," and the three ships came to, a short distance from shore. A landing party of Marines and sailors was immediately made ready and despatched ashore to destroy all villages in the vicinity. This force landed shortly after six o'clock in the morning, and remained ashore until mid-afternoon when they returned, after having destroyed seven villages and inflicting severe punishment upon the natives themselves.

(1860)

Early in this year, the native Africans again became troublesome, and the Americans at Kissembo (Angola, Portuguese West Africa) were in need of protection. Commander Thomas W. Brent, in the sloop *Marion*, was at Kabenda, and, having been advised of the state of affairs at Kissembo, proceeded to that place, where he arrived on the 29th of February. On the following day, March 1st, he detailed the Marine Guard of his vessel and a detachment of sailors, and despatched them ashore as a guard for the protection of lives and property. This force returned to the ship the following morning as their presence was deemed no longer necessary. This action proved inopportune, however, for on the following day, March 3, the Americans ashore signaled the *Marion* for the Marines, but they were not landed until the 4th, when they remained ashore for a few hours and then returned to the ship. Commander Fitzroy, in H.M.S. *Falcon*, was also present, and landed some of his force at the request of English citizens.

(Africa)

(1904)

Tangier was the scene of difficulties on this occasion. The Bandit Raisouli, had captured several hostages, who were being held with an apparent endeavor to embroil the Italian government in his quarrel with the Sultan of Morocco. The whole state of affairs was not conducive of allaying the fears of Christians residing in Tangiers, who were apprehensive of an outbreak against them.

In view of these circumstances, Rear Admiral French E. Chadwick, U.S. Navy, was ordered to proceed with his squadron to Tangiers "to mark the sense of the gravity of the situation on the part of our government." He arrived off Tangier late in May, and in company with the American Consul General, Mr. Gummere, called upon the minister of foreign affairs for Morocco.

The American Consul evidently thought that the situation warranted the establishment of a suitable Marine guard at the Consulate, to which the Admiral apparently agreed, and a guard was so established and maintained from May 30th to June 26th, inclusive, when they were withdrawn. This guard was taken from the flagship Brooklyn, the Marines of which were commanded by Captain John T. Myers, U.S. Marine Corps.

References: Squadron, Coast of Africa, Commodore M.C. Perry, Apr. 10, 1843 to Apr. 29, 1845, Navy Archives; Logs of Decatur, Macedonian, Porpoise, Saratoga, Marion and Brooklyn; A & N Reg., June 25, 1904, 5; Marine Corps Archives; McClellan's Hist. U.S. Marine Corps.

ARGENTINA
(1833)

Insurrection, in what is now the Argentine Republic, dates back to the 16th Century, when Alvar Nunez the Spanish Governor was deposed by the followers of Martinez Irala, and later shipped to Spain as a prisoner. Since this early date many revolutions have taken place for the control of the government. In October of this year one of these uprisings was in progress, and it became so violent as to necessitate a landing by United States naval forces for the protection of American citizens and those of other foreign countries not represented by naval forces in these waters.

Commander John P. Zantzinger, U.S. Navy, in the _Natchez_ was at Buenos Ayres when this uprising took place, but was under orders to take his departure for another port. The United States was not represented in this country by either a diplomatic officer, or a consular agent, and Mr. Daniel Gowland, of the American firm of Daniel Gowland and Company, assumed the responsibilities of representing all citizens of the United States who resided in the city of Buenos Ayres. On the 16th of October he addressed a letter to Commander Zantzinger, in which he expressed keen regret that the American man-of-war was to depart so soon, and the belief that, if the Commodore (Woolsey), was aware of the local conditions, he would retain the _Natchez_ in the harbor.

Commander Zantzinger communicated with Commodore M. T. Woolsey, on the flagship _Lexington_, which was at Montevideo, furnished him with a copy of Mr. Gowland's letter together with a petition signed by American and English merchants, suggesting that his vessel, the _Natchez_ be retained at Buenos Ayres, at least until another American ship should arrive to relieve it, for the protection of the interests of the United States. The Commodore, agreeing with this suggestion, set sail for the troubled area and arrived there on the 21st.

After his arrival and upon familiarizing himself with all of the conditions in the city, Commodore Woolsey deemed it advisable to have some one on shore to look after the interests of his Government, since the United States was not represented at the time by any political agent. Accordingly, he selected Commander Isaac McKeever of the _Lexington_ as

(Argentina)

such representative, and ordered him to reside ashore, until further instructed. Commander McKeever took up his residence on shore the same day, called upon the President, arranged for a salute to be exchanged between the Lexington and the Argentine authorities, obtained such facts about the revolution as practicable, and reported this information to the Commodore.

Conditions ashore remained about the same from day to day, with occasional sporadic outbursts of musketry throughout the city until the 31st of October, when the outbreak became general, and the Commodore deemed it necessary to order an armed party ashore to protect foreign interests. At 3:30 in the afternoon of this date, a force of 43 officers, Marines and sailors proceeded on shore, and were placed under the direct command of Commander McKeever for such disposition as he might deem necessary or advisable. This detachment remained ashore until the 15th of November when, tranquility having been restored, they returned to their ship.

(1852)

This year was ushered in by the advent of another revolution in the political affairs of the republic. The city of Buenos Ayres was invested by land by an allied army from the revolting provinces and Brazil, while by sea a cordon of sloops of war hovered near, and all were in a state of readiness to turn their guns on the beleaguered city when so ordered by the allied leader. General Juan Manuel Rosas had gone out to head his army, and to lead them against the allied forces. The situation was tense, and the populace were in a state of expectancy fraught with impending disaster.

About this time Commodore Isaac McKeever, in his flagship Congress, arrived at Montevideo where he received dispatches from the American Charge' de Affaires, John S. Pendleton, at Buenos Ayres, acquainting him with the state of affairs in that city. Commodore McKeever felt that his presence at the latter place was urgently needed, and that probably additional Marines might be necessary if a landing be required for the protection of the interests of the United States. Accordingly, he ordered the Marine Guard of

(Argentina)

the Congress, under Brevet Captain Algernon S. Taylor and Second Lieutenant George Holmes, to proceed to Buenos Ayres. The Commodore also sailed for that city, and, upon arrival, transferred his pennant to the Jamestown, which was lying in the harbor off Buenos Ayres at the time. On the 2nd of February a meeting was called of all the accredited Diplomatic Corps present, to consider ways and means for the protection of their nationals, and Commodore McKeever, the British admiral and senior naval officers of France, Sardinia and Sweden were invited to attend. At this conference it was decided to apply to the authorities to land such forces as might be necessary under the circumstances.

The following day, February 3rd, scattered forces of Rosas' cavalry began entering the city, and a little later it was learned that they had been defeated by the allied forces investing the city. Renewed alarm was now felt for the safety of foreign citizens, and an immediate answer to the application to land troops was urged - which was given. Commodore McKeever pressed into service the American steamer Manuelita Rosas, loaded her with the Marines of the Congress and Jamestown, ordered her into the inner harbor, and landed the Marines by the use of flat boats from H.B.M. frigate Centaur, which had been loaned to the Marines through the kindness of Admiral Henderson.

The Marines of the Jamestown were commanded by Second Lieutenant John R. F. Tattnall, and combined with those of the Congress, formed guards at the residences of the Charge de Affaires, the Consul Joseph Graham, and that of Messrs. Zimmerman, Frazier and Company, who conducted the largest American mercantile house in the city, and in whose residence Commodore McKeever was a guest. The British and French forces were distributed in a similar manner, and the whole foreign detachment so situated as to be enabled to concentrate at a given point in a minimum of time when required.

Late this same evening (3rd) advices were received that General Justo Jose Urquiza, the allied commander, had defeated General Rosas, and that the latter's army was

(Argentina)

completely dispersed. Based upon this information, the authorities sought the services of the Diplomatic Corps to solicit a stay of the onward march of the conquering allied forces into the city. They agreed, and proceeded to Palermo where they awaited General Urquiza. However, they were unable to communicate with him until the following day when he arrived at Palermo, and upon being advised of the state of affairs, readily agreed to withhold his army, sending only a small force to restore order.

In the meantime several stores had been rifled by a band of pillagers bent upon plundering the city. These mounted pillagers came upon a party of Marines and sailors, under Midshipman Walker, who were patrolling the streets to prevent the sacking of the city, charged and fired upon them but providentially none were harmed by their bullets or the charge. The Marines returned the fire of the pillagers, and four of the robbers fell, two being killed outright and two seriously wounded who died later. This prompt retaliation dispersed the band, and apparently put an end to pillaging outrages in the city.

General Urquiza approved of the landing of the foreign troops, their action in firing upon those bent upon pillage, and requested that these forces remain until such time as he had perfected arrangements for the proper policing of the city and had reestablished tranquility. Commodore McKeever states, relative to the service rendered by the American Marines: "Great credit is due to our gallant Marines for their share in the restoration of comparative safety to life and property. They were under the command of Captain Taylor of the Congress and Lieutenant Tattnall of the Jamestown. * * *" General Rosas, after his defeat at the hands of General Urquiza is said to have entered the city in disguise, and made his escape in the night to H.B.M. Centaur, and later on a steamer bound for England.

On the 7th of February, believing that the allied force was in all respects able to maintain order and tranquility, the American Charge' addressed himself to the Provisional Governor, Senor Vicente Lopez, relative to the advisability of withdrawing the American Marines, to which the latter replied that: "* * * the longer presence in the

(Argentina)

City of the United States Marines seems unnecessary, but that you are at liberty to withdraw them to their vessels, whenever you may find a suitable opportunity. * * *"

In accordance with the desires of the Provisional Governor, the Marines were withdrawn on the 13th of February and returned aboard their respective ships.

On the 11th of September of this same year another outbreak occurred which necessitated the landing of another detachment of American Marines. This new outbreak was caused by reason of the action of General Urquiza in deposing the officials of the provisional government whom he had previously appointed, and the assuming himself of the office of Governor of that Province. Just prior to this insurrection, Commodore McKeever arrived at Montevideo, and on the 3rd of August despatched Captain Samuel W. Downing, in the Jamestown, to Buenos Ayres to observe conditions. He arrived, and was present when the outbreak occurred. This affair did not reach the proportions that the earlier one had. Nevertheless, a Marine guard at the American Consulate was deemed advisable, and on the 17th of September a guard was so landed for the protection of American interests. The exact date these Marines returned to their ship is as yet unascertainable. However, it is believed to be sometime in April, 1853.

(1890)

In July of this year still another revolution was in progress in the province of Buenos Ayres, and a small detachment of Marines was landed for the protection of the American Consulate and the residence of the Minister, John R.G. Pitkin. These Marines were landed from the Tallapoosa, and remained ashore until July 30th, when they were withdrawn and returned to their ship.

References: Kirkpatrick, The Argentine Republic, Ch.II; Captain's Letters, 1833, #15, 16, 18, 20, 21, and 39, with enclosures, Navy Archives; Brazil Sqd. Letters, 1852-53, #43, 44, 45, 55, 58, 66 and 67, with enclosures, Navy Archives; Logs of Lexington, Jamestown, Congress, and Tallapoosa; St. Dept. Archives; Marine Corps Archives.

B E R I N G   S E A
(Seal Poaching)

(1891)

Seal poaching in the Bering Sea had become so serious a matter that there was danger of their becoming extinct, and the United States government decided that remedial measures were necessary to prevent their extermination by the persons engaged in the employment of sealing. Great Britain had expressed a like decision, and agreed to cooperate with the United States in ending this evil practice.

The United States Government decided to send some small armed vessels into the area, and selected Commander C.S. Cotton, U.S. Navy, as commander of the forces. The Pacific Coast Steamship Company's vessel, Al-Ki, was chartered as one of the ships to comprise the squadron, and, on being provided with a detachment of Marines, under Captain Henry C. Cochrane, she sailed from Mare Island on the 22nd of June and arrived in the Bering Sea July 2nd. The Thetis arrived on the 3rd, followed on the 8th by the Mohican (Commander Cotton) which in turn was followed by the Alert the next day, and the Marion on the 14th of August. With the exception of the Thetis, all of these vessels had Marine Guards, with a total strength of 5 officers and 113 enlisted Marines.

The British Government selected H.M.S. Nymphe, Pheasant and the Porpoise, to cooperate with the American vessels, and they joined on July 7th, 12th, and 27th, respectively, each with a guard of British marines on board.

Two revenue cutters, the Corwin and Rush, also joined the other American vessels. These were employed to cruise the seal herd area, and notify all persons engaged in sealing, whaling or fishing of the contents of the President's proclamation, and the orders of the British Government relative to the fur seal fisheries. The Al-Ki was designated as "harbor and prison ship" at Ounalaska, and the crews of all vessels seized were transferred to her custody, pending final disposition of their cases.

Owing to the notification distributed by the Cutters, and the determined efforts of the American and British armed vessels, but four seizures were necessary for

(Bering Sea)

infringement of the rules promulgated by the proclamation and the orders of the British Government. These four were the British schooners E.B. Marvin and Otto, and the American Schooners La Nifa and Ethel. The English ships were sent to Victoria, and the American ships to Sitka, Alaska, for adjudication and disposal. The La Nifa and Ethel were towed by the Al-Ki the whole distance of about 1,200 miles to Sitka, and were furnished with a Marine Guard, who kept Captain Cochrane advised of conditions aboard them by signals during the trip.

The Marines of the squadron were organized into boats' crews, and did all of the boarding of sealing vessels, and other work requiring the use of small boats, besides their regular routine drills and target practice. They gave exhibition drills at Sitka and at Lliuliuk, which were appreciated by the inhabitants, and many complimentary remarks were made regarding the soldierly appearance of the United States Marines.

In the latter part of September the weather became stormy, and the sealers ceased operations for the season and departed for home ports. The work of the squadron had been completed and, on October 5th, it also headed for home waters, arriving at Mare Island on the 14th, having covered approximately 6,600 miles since its departure on June 22nd.

An incident, well worth recording, happened about a month prior to the start of the Al-Ki on her return voyage. Much trouble had been occasioned on the cruise by mutinous manifestations of the crew, who were foreigners and "union men", especially of the engineers' department. The aid of the civil law already had been invoked, on two occasions, to settle disputes between the Captain and his crew. On the third, and last, occasion - that of September 9th - the "Skipper" was apparently at his wits end and appealed to Captain Cochrane for information as to whether he could depend upon the Marines in the event that the "worst comes to worst." Captain Cochrane informed him that: "Yes, you can set every one of them on the beach, firemen and all, and we'll take the ship to San Francisco." The Captain of the Al-Ki reported to his employers that Captain Cochrane's declaration ended his troubles.

References: Sec. Navy An. Rep., 1891, 620-621; Logs of Alert, Marion, Mohican and Thetis; Marine Corps Archives.

C H I L E

(1891)

The first conquest of Chile is believed to have been that of the Inca Tupac-Yapanqui which took place in the beginning of the 15th century. This belief is based on the finding of remains, including stones on which is inscribed writing that is as yet undeciphered, indicating a population that existed in remote times.

The Incas ruled for about a century when the local Curacos became virtually independent. However, it was not long before other conquerors appeared and Almagro, Valdivia, and Mendoza (the first named being most notable), tried to force their regimes on the people.

After nearly three centuries had elapsed, San Martin, at the head of a joint expedition of Argentine and Chilean forces, crossed the Andes and in a brilliant campaign, freed Chile, whose independence was proclaimed on February 12, 1818. The United States recognized her as an independent state four years later. Bernardo O'Higgins, as political director, headed this new government until he was deposed by a revolution in 1823. Following O'Higgins' deposition, mutinies, assassinations, and dictatorships took place in rapid succession.

This reign of terror was not concluded until the Battle of Lircai (April 17, 1830), when the conservative faction triumphed. Succeeding years brought little change, for they, too, were marked by bloody contests and revolutions between the different factions.

During the conflict between Spain and Peru in 1864, Chile also declared war against Spain. While this war was in progress, the bombardment (by the Spanish) of the unfortified port of Valparaiso in 1866 took place, and upon this incident is based the claim that Chile is the only American State to have suffered a loss of blood in defense of the Monroe Doctrine.

(Chile)

In this year (1891), the people of this revolutionary-ridden republic were again in a state of open insurrection against the faction then supposed to be controlling the government. Conditions were in a deplorable state, due to the capture in August, of Valparaiso by the forces of the Congressional party. Foreigners residing within the boundaries of the republic, especially those living in the captured city, were in great danger of losing their lives and property. Even foreign legations and consulates were in danger of being violated.

During the course of this revolution, a bitter feeling against the United States arose, due, it is believed, to the false and malicious accusations put forth at Iquique and later at Valparaiso in reference to the action of the Navy of the United States.

The American Minister, Patrick Egan, concurred in the belief that foreign armed forces were necessary, not only for the moral effect on the insurrectionists, but as a means of protection for Americans and American interests.

In the latter part of March, Rear Admiral George Brown had been ordered to Chilean waters as the relief of Rear Admiral William P. McCann, and was issued definite and detailed instructions for his guidance in view of the unsettled state of affairs in the latter country. Admiral Brown proceeded in the San Francisco, and in company with the Baltimore, was present at Valparaiso when that city was captured by the revolutionists.

The American Minister applied to Admiral Brown for a suitable guard for the Legation, and his request was granted. A detachment of 36 Marines and 36 sailors, under the command of Captain William S. Muse, U.S.M.C., was landed on the 28th of August and remained until the 30th, when they were withdrawn.

About six weeks after the withdrawal of the Marine Guard from the American Consulate, an affair took place which assumed grave aspects – one which merited the landing of Marines to again protect American citizens, and

(Chile)

indicated in no unmistakable terms the extreme ill-feeling that the Chileans harbored toward the Americans. The affair referred to, was the attack, on October 16th, in the City of Valparaiso, on members of a liberty party of the Baltimore. However, Admiral Brown, because of this extreme ill-feeling, and believing that the matter could be more appropriately handled through diplomatic representation by the United States Department of State, deemed it inadvisable to use the Marine landing force at his disposal.

On this date a number of men belonging to the Baltimore, went on shore in uniform for liberty, in accordance with the universal practice prevailing on board the ships of war in foreign ports. Two weeks had passed since the surrender of Valparaiso, and the city was quiet. Other foreign war ships had already given liberty, and no reason existed for withholding a like privilege from the men of the Baltimore. At 6 p.m. the men had been ashore about four hours, and the testimony is that they were then orderly, sober, and well behaved.

The first encounter appears to have taken place at this time between one of the members of the liberty party and a Chilean, who spat in his face. The sailor knocked the Chilean down and was immediately set upon, with his companion, another of the Baltimore's crew, by an angry crowd. The two sailors took refuge in a passing street car. They were dragged from the car by the crowd. One of them, Petty Officer Charles Riggin, was stabbed, and left to die in the street. His companion, Talbot, an apprentice, escaped, but was afterwards arrested, catgut nippers were put on his wrists, and he was struck again and again by the police on his way to prison.

Another Petty Officer, Johnson, then in a neighboring house, seeing Riggin lying helpless in the street, went to his assistance. The crowd now left. Finding Riggin still breathing, Johnson took him in his arms to carry him to a drug store nearby. At this moment a squad of Chilean police, with fixed bayonets, came up the street. When at close quarters they fired at Johnson, being so near that his face was blackened by this discharge. One shot entered

(Chile)

Riggin's neck and shoulder, inflicting a death wound. Another shot passed through Johnson's clothing.

    The affair of the street car was only one of many simultaneous attacks made upon the <u>Baltimore's</u> men. The attacks lasted for an hour. They were not confined to one locality, but occurred at several widely separated points in the city. In many instances the American sailors were in restaurants and hotels, quietly getting supper when attacked by crowds numbering from 25 to 200 men. The part borne by the police in these attacks is shown by the report. Thirty-six of the <u>Baltimore's</u> men were arrested and taken to prison, being subjected on the way to treatment of the utmost brutality. Catgut nippers were placed on their wrists, and in the case of one man, McWilliams, a lasso was thrown about his neck. Williams, another apprentice, 19 years of age, was arrested by a mounted policeman who put the nippers around his wrists and then started his horse into a gallop, throwing the boy down. Coal-heaver Quigley, in trying to escape from the mob was struck with a sword by a police officer. Petty Officer Hamilton was dragged to prison dangerously wounded and unconscious and his companions, attempting to relieve his sufferings were threatened with blows from musket butts, and compelled to desist.

    Coal-heaver Turnbull received 18 wounds in the back, two of which penetrated his lungs and subsequently caused his death. Other men were seriously injured and several of the wounds were caused by bayonet thrusts, clearly showing the participation of the police. As a result of the attacks, two of the men, Riggin and Turnbull, died, and eighteen others were more or less disabled by wounds.

    At the examination immediately following the arrest, which was conducted secretly, a request was made of the authorities by Captain Schley to allow one of his officers to be present in court. The request was denied. Before the men were discharged they were required to sign a paper in Spanish. A court official, whom one of the men asked what might be the meaning of the paper, declared that it was a mere form, stating that the signer had not been engaged in the trouble.

(Chile)

The members of the liberty party during the attack were without arms and therefore defenseless. Of the thirty-six men arrested and examined, all were discharged, there being no proof of any violation of the peace on their part. The judicial investigation into the conduct of the men failed to show that a single one was found drunk or disorderly. It is clear that their only offense lay in wearing the uniform of the country to which they belonged.

References: Sec. Navy An. Rep., 1891, 21-30, 618; Logs of Baltimore and San Francisco; St. Dept. Archives; Marine Corps Archives.

CHINA

(1854)

Ts'ung-cheng, the last emperor of the Ming dynasty, ascended the throne in 1627. During his reign English merchants first made their appearance at Canton, which was the only open port in the empire. The country was now torn by internal dissentions, and rebel bands assumed the proportions of armies. They roamed the country, leaving a devastated trail behind. Pirates, also, made their appearance, and infested the coasts. Their number and organization enabled them for a long time to hold the imperial fleet in check.

Canton was the scene of all commercial trading with Europeans. Conditions at this place became so offensive as to cause Great Britain to declare war against China in 1840. The outcome of this war was the ceding of Hong Kong to the British, and the payment of a six million dollar indemnity. Two years later, Sir Henry Pottinger concluded a treaty by which Amoy, Fu-chow, Ningpo and Shanghai were declared open to foreign trade, and an indemnity of twenty-one million dollars was to be paid the British.

Hien-feng ascended the throne in 1850, but the relief looked forward to by the people did not materialize, and they proclaimed a youth, who was said to be the representative of the last emperor of the Ming dynasty, as emperor under the title of T'ien-te. However, another leader, Hung Siu-ts'uan, with a large following, entered the field, and, by the year 1853 had established himself within the walls of Nanking, proclaiming a new dynasty - that of T'ai-p'ing - and nominating himself first emperor under the title of T'ien Wang or "Heavenly King."

During the progress of this internal upheaval foreigners, including Americans, were in grave danger from the marauding hosts of Chinese, but they did not assume an aspect so serious as to necessitate the actual landing of Marines for the protection of Americans until early in 1854, although Marines were standing by off Canton in case their services were required.

Commodore Matthew C. Perry had been commissioned to negotiate a treaty with Japan (see "Japan" in this compilation), and he had selected the port of Shanghai, China, as his base from which to conduct his operations, therefore, the United States was represented by a considerable naval force in Chinese waters when the outbreak occurred which necessitated the landing of American Marines early in this year, 1854.

(China)

Perry had left the sloop *Plymouth*, under Commander John Kelly, at Shanghai, to look after American interests while he was absent with the remainder of his squadron at the port of Yeddo, Japan, on his original mission of negotiating a treaty. The Imperial and Revolutionary forces were engaged in open hostilities in and around Shanghai, and the foreigners were left to protect themselves as best they could. About six o'clock in the evening of April 4th a signal was observed on shore which said: "Want assistance." Commander Kelly immediately directed Lieutenant John Guest to prepare a landing force consisting of the Marine Guard and enough sailors to total 60 men, and proceed ashore to protect Americans. A little later in the same evening an additional force of 11 men was sent ashore to guard the American Mission grounds. The following morning, the 5th, it was observed that the Imperial troops were encroaching upon the Foreign Settlement, and it was desired to drive them away and thereby relieve the possibility of danger which would ensue should the opposing forces open active hostilities.

Great Britain, also had a naval force present at Shanghai and, together with the Americans decided to make a combined landing, and drive the Chinese troops from their position. At about one o'clock in the afternoon, Commander Kelly made ready a force of approximately 60 Marines and sailors, a Howitzer field piece and crew, and taking command of the force himself, proceeded to land. Upon reaching the shore, this force was joined by a British force consisting of about 150 marines and sailors, besides a number of English volunteers and about 30 men from American merchant vessels then lying off Shanghai. The Imperial forces would not evacuate the position they held, and it was necessary to resort to force of arms. The enemy, after sustaining a sharp fire of musketry for some ten minutes, suffered their flank to be turned by the American and British troops, which resulted in a hasty and disordered retreat, on the part of the Chinese, leaving a number of dead and wounded where they fell. By six in the evening they had been driven away from the Settlement, and the combined force had returned to their respective ships, excepting 35 men at the American Consulate and 11 at the American Mission, who remained guarding these placed until the 15th of June when they were withdrawn. During the engagement with the Imperial troops, the Americans suffered casualties of one sailor killed and two Marines and one sailor wounded, while the British force lost about the same number.

(China)

(1855)

Piracy, which had its inception in the 17th century, was still being practiced by some of the Chinese, even though condign punishment had been meted out to them on numerous occasions by American and British armed forces. These pirates were bold, strong, and indefatigable in their operations against merchant shipping. Vessels plying the Coast were plundered, and the most imaginable scenes that can be ascribed to the idea of piracy became realities in the career of these lawless bands. The Imperial Chinese Government not employing the necessary means to end this nefarious practice, foreign vessels were left either to protect themselves, or be protected by naval vessels of their own country.

In view of these conditions, to which was added the internal political strife then in progress, the United States deemed it prudent to maintain several men-of-war in these waters to furnish the protection for its citizens which the Chinese had failed to give. The steam frigate Powhatan, under Captain William J. McCluney, was one of the American naval vessels assigned to this duty. On the 8th of March she put in to Shanghai, where local conditions were found to be in a chaotic state. No landing was necessary, however, until the 19th of May, when the Marine guard, consisting of 41 men, under the command of First Lieutenant James H. Jones, was sent ashore at 3 o'clock in the afternoon. The exact date on which this landing force returned to the ship has not been ascertained, but it is believed to be that of the 21st, from the fact that when it was landed "extra grog", was issued "to Marines," which would indicate duty of more than one day, and furthermore that the Powhatan sailed at 5 o'clock in the evening of the 21st.

In August of this same year, the pirates were active around Hong Kong, and a fleet of their vessels was known to be at Ku Lan, which was not far distant. The Powhatan and the British man-of-war, H.B.M. sloop Rattler, were lying at anchor off Hong Kong, and their commanders conferred relative to attacking and destroying the pirates. Captain McCluney detailed Lieutenant Jones and 26 of his Marines, 66 sailors and 7 naval officers, supplied them with four days provisions "& whiskey," and at 3 o'clock in the afternoon of the 3rd they left the ship to join the force from the British vessel, which took their boats in tow and proceeded on the mission.

The engagement with the pirates took place the following day in Ty-ho Bay. This battle lasted for some hours,

(China)

but resulted in victory for the combined American-British forces. Seventeen pirate junks were captured, another was blown up by the pirates themselves to prevent its capture, and many of the band were taken prisoners. The American casualties numbered 2 Marines and 9 sailors; 3 of the latter being killed in action, while the others were more or less seriously wounded. The two Marines, Privates Adamson and Mullard, later died of their wounds aboard the British hospital ship Hercules, and were buried at Hong Kong. The whole force returned to their ship late in the evening of the 5th, having been absent slightly over 48 hours.

(1856)

Conditions at Canton in the latter part of this year were in an unsettled state, and a clash between British naval forces and the Chinese authorities was momentarily expected. The United States sloop Portsmouth, under the command of Commander Andrew H. Foote, was lying at anchor off Whampoa when, shortly after midnight of October 22nd, Commander Foote received a communication from the American Consul at Canton, Mr. Oliver H. Perry, to the effect that the expected hostilities were imminent, and that an American armed force should be despatched there to protect the interests of the United States. The Commander lost no time in preparing a landing force for this duty. He selected Second Lieutenant William W. Kirkland with 18 of his Marines, 4 naval officers, 60 sailors, the field Howitzer, and taking command of the whole, shoved off at 6:20 a.m. for Canton.

As hostilities progressed between the British and Chinese forces, and the dangers to foreigners became greater, the American force which had already been sent to Canton, was thought inadequate to furnish the protection required by the conditions. Commander William Smith, in command of the sloop Levant, ordered a landing force from his ship, consisting of Second Lieutenant Henry B. Tyler and his Marines, and a detachment of sailors, and on the 27th (October), proceeded to Canton, where he joined the force from the Portsmouth.

Commodore James Armstrong, in his flagship, the steam frigate San Jacinto, arrived off Whampoa shortly before noon of November 12th, and on the 14th ordered Brevet Captain John D. Simms, with 28 of his Marines, to proceed to Canton and join the force under Commander Foote, who was the senior American officer on shore. On the 16th this detachment of Marines returned to the ship. About this time Commander Foote reported aboard the flagship in person for a conference with Commodore Armstrong, relative to withdrawing the Marines

(China)

and sailors from shore, and placing them aboard the *Levant*, which would then be anchored off Canton. This agreement had been reached, and Commander Foote was on his way back to Canton to carry out the plan when, upon arriving abreast of the first fort, his boat was fired upon and it was necessary for him to return to Whampoa.

This unprovoked assault upon an unarmed boat, displaying the American Flag, was too much for the patience of the Commodore, and he immediately proceeded to act. He ordered a landing force from his own vessel, consisting of Captain Simms and his Marines, 6 naval officers, including two surgeons, together with sailors, to total about 150 men, despatched them to the *Portsmouth*, and transferred his broad pennant to the same vessel. In the meantime, both the *Levant* and *Portsmouth* were ordered to prepare to proceed up the river in tow of the steamers *Cumfa* and *Williamette*, respectively. Commander Henry H. Bell, of the *San Jacinto*, was ordered to command the *Levant* owing to the absence of Commander Smith at Canton. The latter named vessel got underway shortly after noon of the 16th, and the *Portsmouth* followed her about 2 hours later. These two vessels had not proceeded far before the four Chinese forts opened fire on them. The *Levant*, in manoeuvering into position, grounded and was thereafter unable to participate in the bombardment.

The fire from the forts was quite accurate, and the *Portsmouth* was hit several times. Some of her rigging was carried away, and one shot penetrated the stern frame, badly wounding one of the Marines. The engagement was continued until dusk, when all firing ceased - the *Portsmouth* having expended 230 shells and several stands of grape. Herculean efforts were employed to get the *Levant* off the bar, and to move her into position for engaging the forts. These efforts were finally successful, and shortly after midnight of the 17th, she was ready to join the further bombardment. On that date the Commodore was taken ill and returned to the *San Jacinto* at Whampoa, leaving Commander Foote in command of both vessels, and all subsequent operations against the forts.

Commander Foote now laid plans for continuing the bombardment of the forts with both vessels, and also made the necessary arrangements for a landing force of Marines and sailors to be sent ashore when the ships had prepared the way by silencing the enemy's fire, or at least when it had so slackened as to make the venture not too hazardous. The

(China)

17th, 18th and 19th were devoted to these preparations, to negotiations with the governor of Canton, which were unsuccessful, and by the 20th everything was in readiness for what was hoped would be the final assault.

At six-thirty in the morning of the 20th, the _Levant_ and _Portsmouth_ opened a heavy fire on the Barrier and Fiddler's forts, which was returned with vigor by the enemy. However, the fire from the American vessels was so accurate that by about seven-thirty the enemy's fire slackened considerably, and Commander Foote deemed the time opportune for a landing. A force consisting of the Marines from the three vessels, under Captain Simms, and Lieutenants Kirkland and Tyler, several naval officers, detachments of sailors totalling about 280 men, and three howitzers, were all standing by for the order which would start them for shore. Commander Bell commanded the force from the _San Jacinto_ and _Portsmouth_, and Commander Smith those of the _Levant_, while Commander Foote, being senior, commanded the whole.

The whole force was now embarked in the ships' boats, and headed for the shore. At eight-fifty the force, under cover of the guns of the two ships, landed near one of the forts, and soon it was in their possession, with the American Flag flying over its ramparts. The casualties of the Chinese were severe - many being killed outright, and a greater number being wounded during the engagement and while retreating from the fort. The spiking of the guns and the destruction of the fortress now commenced. The enemy, with a force of about 3000 men, attempted to retake the fort three different times during the day, but they were repulsed on all occasions by Captain Simms and 60 Marines, and on the third foray the Marines routed the Chinese completely.

The landing force remained in this fort until four o'clock the following morning, when they returned alongside the _Portsmouth_, where they were held to await orders for further landings. The _Levant_ was now towed to a position from which she could bring her guns to bear on Fiddlers fort, and together with the _Portsmouth_ opened a brisk fire on the enemy position. This was continued until about eight-thirty, when the landing force was towed to the beach by the _Cumfa_. This force landed shortly before nine, under cover of the bombardment, and by nine-thirty the fort had been captured and the American Flag raised over it. The guns were now spiked and the fort dismantled. In the afternoon the landing force crossed the river, landed near the Island fort, and captured it, while the ships continued the bombardment of the remaining forts. Early in the morning of the 22nd, the work of reducing the other forts was commenced. The ships opened fire at five o'clock, and a half hour later,

(China)

the landing force, under Commander Foote, crossed the river under a heavy fire, landed near fort Number four, and in less than two hours, it too, was in the possession of the Americans. All of the Barrier forts having been captured, as well as Fiddlers fort, the landing party returned to their ships at two-thirty in the afternoon.

During the fighting up to and including the 22nd, the Americans suffered casualties of six killed (sailors), and twenty wounded, six of the wounded being Marines. The losses on the enemy's side could not be accurately ascertained, however, they were known to be severe, both in killed and wounded. The Chinese defended the forts with approximately 5000 officers and men, while the American force (landing party) did not quite reach 300, officers and men, who were pitted against forts with granite walls seven feet in thickness, and an armament of 168 heavy guns, some of which had a bore of eleven inches in diameter.

On the afternoon of the 23rd a large party of Marines and sailors was despatched on shore to occupy the forts "on the right hand" side of the river, tear down the walls, roll the guns into the river, and otherwise complete their destruction in such manner as to preclude the possibility of their ever being used again. This work continued until the 6th of December, when the destruction was complete and the entire landing force returned aboard their respective ships. Shortly before seven o'clock that evening, both vessels were towed down the river to the anchorage at Whampoa.

(1859)

In May of the previous year a British force captured the Taku Forts, and Lord Elgin started for Peking. At Tientsin, however, imperial commissioners persuaded him to conclude a treaty on the spot, which treaty it was agreed should be ratified the following year. Sir Frederick Bruce was despatched from England on the mission for ratification of the treaty, but had to return, unsuccessful, due to the fact that while attempting to pass the Taku Forts, he and his escort of vessels were fired upon, and the expedition was compelled to return.

This incident seemed to embolden the Tartars in their conduct toward all foreigners, and was the apparent signal for the perpetration of many indignities upon them, among whom were Americans. This was the state of affairs when Captain William C. Nicholson, in the steam frigate *Mississippi*, arrived off Woosung in the latter part of July, 1859. The American Consul at Shanghai, William L.G. Smith, acquainted Captain Nicholson with the conditions and, apparently, requested or suggested, the advisability of

(China)

sending an armed party to Shanghai for the protection of the interests of the United States. Early in the morning of the 31st, Captain Nicholson ordered a detachment of Marines (presumably under command of First Lieutenant Jacob Read), and sailors to the number of 60 officers and men, also a boat howitzer, the whole under Lieutenant Roger N. Stemble, and despatched them to Shanghai in tow of the English steamer Carthage. This force remained at Shanghai until the 2nd of August, when it was withdrawn.

(1866)

Hien-feng died in the summer of 1861, leaving the throne to his son, T'ung-chi, a child of five years, whose mother, Tsz'e Hsi, had been raised from the place of favorite concubine to that of Imperial Consort. The legitimate empress, Tsz'e An, was childless, and the two dowagers became joint regents. The concluding of peace with the allies, England, France and Russia, together with the death of Hien-feng and the ascension of his son to the throne, appeared to be the signal for a renewal of the campaign against the T'ai-p'ings, and benefiting by the friendly feelings of the British authorities, engendered by the return of amicable relations, the Chinese government succeeded in enlisting Major Charles George Gordon, of the Royal Engineers, in their services. He supplanted an American named Ward, and in a surprisingly short time formed the Chinese troops into a formidable army and without delay took the field against the rebels. His advent met with much success, and in July, 1864, the imperialists gained possession of Nanking. T'ien Wang, the Rebel leader, committed suicide, and those of his followers who escaped dispersed throughout the country.

Even though the rebels had been dispersed, certain War Lords still made forays into imperial territory, cities and towns, committing diverse depredations, and harassing foreigners who might be within their sphere of operations. Such was the general state of affairs when, in this year, the American Consul at New Chwang, Francis P. Knight, was molested and assaulted by a party of dissolute characters, the leader of which was known by the name of "Sword Rack Hoo." Rear Admiral Henry H. Bell, commanding the Asiatic Squadron, despatched Commander Robert Townsend, in the Washusett, to the scene for the purpose of securing the arrest and punishment of the parties who were engaged in the outrage.

Commander Townsend arrived off New Chwang about the middle of June and, on the 20th, sent a landing force

(China)

numbering 50 Marines and sailors, under the command of Lieutenant John W. Philip, to obtain all information available relative to the assault, and to arrange for the arrest and conviction of its perpetrators. It appeared that the local Chinese authorities could, and would take into custody all of those implicated, with the exception of the leader, whom the authorities seemed powerless to arrest. Commander Townsend was unwilling to permit this individual, above all others, to escape his just dues for the unprovoked attack on an American consular officer, and, on the 25th, despatched 100 Marines and sailors, under Lieutenant Philip, with explicit orders, we can imagine, to bring back his man. At any rate, Philip returned with his party that evening, bringing the chief of the "Sword Racks" with him. "Sword Rack Hoo" was placed on trial the following day, and Lieutenant Philip, with a detachment of about 25 men went ashore each day until the 29th to make certain Hoo did not escape until after the trial.

On July 7th, the 22 "sword racks" having been tried and punishment awarded, the entire number were turned over to the Chinese authorities, and the Wachusett sailed, taking the Consul to Chefoo. The Wachusett then proceeded to Tung Chow Foo, arriving there on the 12th. On the 14th, Commander Townsend wishing to consult with the authorities on shore, detailed 100 Marines and sailors, under Lieutenant Philip, to accompany him. They landed at 11 in the morning and returned at 6 in the evening. Commander Townsend next visited Shanghai, arriving there the 26th. While at anchor here on August 9th, a serious fire was observed from the Wachusett, in the direction of Old Shanghai, and 1 officer and 46 men were immediately sent on shore to render assistance. They landed shortly after 3 o'clock in the morning, and returned around 6, the fire having been extinguished.

The United States Consul-General, Mr. Seward, and the Interpreter, Mr. Jenkins, were desirous of proceeding to Chinkiang, so Commander Townsend offered passage on the Wachusett, which was accepted. They went aboard her on the morning of the 12th of August, and disembarked at 5:30 on the evening of the 14th; Lieutenant Philip, with 25 men, acting as escort. The Consul-General had departed less than seven hours when all aboard the Wachusett were suddenly plunged in grief, and a pall of sadness hovered over the American vessel. This was occasioned by the death of Commander Townsend at 1:40 in the morning of the 15th, of congestion of the brain. The Wachusett got underway and stood down the river to Shanghai, where the remains of Commander Townsend were laid to rest on the evening of the 16th.

(China)

Full military honors were accorded, and 7 one minute guns were fired from the vessel he had so ably commanded.

(1894)

This year witnessed the outbreak of hostilities with Japan, due to the immemorable rivalry between these two countries for influence in Corea. In the 16th century a prolonged war was fought, which ended with the failure of Japan to make good her footing on the mainland. In more modern times, 1875, 1882 and 1884, Japan had repeatedly sent expeditions to Corea, and had fostered the growth of a progressive party in Seoul. The difficulties of 1884 were settled by the convention of Tientsin, wherein it was agreed that in the event of future intervention each should inform the other if it were decided to despatch troops to the peninsula. Nine years later the occasion arose. A serious rebellion induced the Corean government to apply for military assistance from China. Early in June of the present year a small force of Chinese troops was sent to Asan, and Japan, duly informed, replied by furnishing her minister at Seoul with an escort, rapidly following up this step by despatching 5000 troops under General Oshima.

Japan now proposed that the two powers unite to suppress the disturbance, and inaugurate certain reforms. China considered that these measures should be left to Corea herself. This controversy continued, until about the middle of July, when it became apparent that, unless China was willing to abandon all claims over Corea, war with Japan was inevitable. At Seoul the issue was forced by the Japanese minister, who delivered an ultimatum to the Corean government on July 20th. On the 23rd the palace was forcibly occupied by the Japanese, and on August 1st war was declared.

Rear Admiral Charles C. Carpenter, commanding the Asiatic Squadron, was issued instructions relative to providing utmost protection for American interests, due to the unsettled conditions in consequence of the war. During the latter part of the year, when the Japanese army approached quite near to Peking, there was occasion for great excitement. Riots occurred with frequency, foreigners were unwelcome, and the foreign diplomatic representatives were apprehensive for their own safety. Admiral Carpenter, who was on his flagship, the *Baltimore*, at Nagasaki, Japan, at the time, received a cablegram to proceed at once, and place his Marine guard at the disposal of the American Minister, Colonel Charles Denby, at Peking, to protect the

(China)

Legation. The Baltimore sailed on the 2nd of December, and arrived at Chefoo on the afternoon of the 4th. Preparations were immediately instituted for the Marines, under Captain George F. Elliott, to embark aboard the steamer Yiksang, and proceed for Tientsin, for further transfer to Peking if required. Captain Elliott went on board with his detachment about 7 o'clock in the evening of the 4th, and started for Taku. However, he was later compelled to transfer from the Yiksang to a tug to complete the journey to the latter place. Here he engaged rail transportation for himself and men to Tientsin, and after riding in open cars for over two hours arrived at his destination, late in the evening of the 6th, all nearly frozen because of the cold weather and lack of protection.

As soon as he arrived at Tientsin, Captain Elliott reported aboard the Monocacy, which was lying at anchor in the river. The Marines had actually made a landing, even though they were prevented from proceeding on to Peking, due to an edict issued by the Emperor forbidding foreign troops to enter the Chinese capital. Other foreign nations were represented by vessels and detachments of marines, all in readiness to proceed to Peking to protect their legations.

(1895)

This year was ushered in and found the Marines still at Tientsin where they were awaiting eventualities. In February Admiral Carpenter ordered that Captain Elliott be instructed to proceed to Peking, for the purpose of conferring with Colonel Denby relative to arrangements for housing facilities, and the feeding of the men, should their presence there be required. Also, to learn the intentions of the missionaries should the Japanese invade the Pichili district, and move on the capital. Twenty-five thousand Chinese troops lined the route from Tientsin to Peking, and rail transportation was impossible. Not to be outdone by these obstacles, this resourceful and experienced officer of American Marines, Captain Elliott, finally secured a horse, and made the trip of over 80 miles to Peking in two days.

During his stay in Peking, Captain Elliott together with Paymaster Cowie, U.S. Navy, acted as military attaches upon the occasion of Colonel Denby's audience with the Emperor of China. Prince Lung begged Colonel Denby, in the name of the Emperor, to draw up a request to the Japanese asking them to receive a peace commissioner. Pending these negotiations, it was not desired to despatch the American Marines to the capital, and Captain Elliott returned to the Monocacy at Tientsin. Peace having been declared on the

(China) 32

10th of May, Captain Elliott and his Marines were ordered to return to their own vessel, the Baltimore, which was then at Nagasaki. They left Tientsin on the 16th, proceeded aboard the Concord and Yorktown, and rejoined their ship on the 20th of the same month.

(1898)

Shortly after the close of the Chinese-Japanese War, a great reform movement began throughout China. The foreign powers apparently underrated this reactionary movement against the aggressive spirit of Western civilization. Foreign methods which had been amply illustrated by the war, had produced a considerable impression upon the people of China. From the treaty ports Chinese newspapers spread the fermentation of new ideas far into the interior. Early in the year, the Emperor, having emancipated himself from the control of the Dowager-Empress, summoned several reform leaders to Peking, requesting their council. The Empress resisted the reform movement in every possible way, and in the middle of September a report became current that the Emperor intended to seize and deport her to the interior. The Empress, no doubt, was cognizant of this plan of the Emperor, and saw her opportunity to regain control of the government. The Emperor had neglected to inculcate the army with his ideas of reform, which fact was known to the Empress, and on the night of the 20th she saw to it that soldiers were surreptitiously permitted to enter the Emperor's palace. He was seized, made a prisoner, and the following day compelled to issue an edict restoring the empress to the regency. In the following month, October, the reaction to the reform movement had already been accompanied by such a recrudescence of anti-foreign feeling that foreign ministers at Peking were apprehensive for the safety of their nationals, themselves, and their Legations.

Mr. Edwin H. Conger relieved Colonel Denby as United States Minister to China, prior to this coup de main. When this happened he considered that a Marine Guard should be established at the Legation in Peking and the Consulate at Tientsin. The American Consul at the latter place was James W. Ragsdale, who, it appeared, shared in this belief. Admiral George Dewey was commanding the Asiatic Station, and when the question was put up to him for decision, he agreed with the Minister and issued the necessary instructions for the guards to be sent. The cruisers Baltimore, Boston, and Raleigh were then in Chinese waters, and Captain Frank Wildes (Boston), being the senior naval officer, directed that First Lieutenant Robert McM. Dutton, commanding the Marines of his vessel, together with a certain number of Marines from all three ships, be despatched to Peking. On the 4th of November, the detachment, consisting of 5 men from the

(China)

Boston, 5 from the Raleigh and 8 from the Baltimore, proceeded to Peking, and established the Legation Guard. On the 12th of the same month, Lieutenant John Gibson, U.S.N., of the Boston, was detailed to command the Marine Guard at the Consulate at Tientsin. This guard consisted of 30 Marines taken from the same three ships, and it proceeded on this date. Each guard was provided with full equipment, including one Gatling gun with a large supply of ammunition.

(1899)

At the beginning of this year, conditions not having improved to any great extent, the American Marines were still on duty guarding the Legation at Peking, and the Consulate at Tientsin. However, the unsettled state of affairs then existing was confidently expected to take a turn for better in the near future. This expectancy was well founded, and by the middle of March they had so improved as to make a Marine Guard no longer a necessity. Consequently, both the Legation and Consulate guards were withdrawn on the 15th of March. They proceeded by train to Shanghai, where they reported aboard the Monocacy and Zafiro the 17th for further transfer to their respective ships.

(1900)

The reactionary tide which began in 1898, continued to rise during the latter part of 1899, and into the present year when it may be said to have reached its climax in the destruction of several Christian villages, whose converts were massacred, and the murder of two English missionaries, in the latter part of May and the first two days of June. The origin of the "Boxer" movement is obscure, but its literal translation is: "The fist of righteous harmony." Whether the Empress Tsz'e Hsi and her Manchu advisers had deliberately set themselves to avert the danger by deflecting a revolutionary movement into anti-foreign channels, or whether with Oriental heedlessness they had allowed it to grow until they were powerless to control it, they had unquestionably resolved to take it under their protection before the foreign representatives at Peking had realized its gravity. Threats against the foreigners went on increasing - the Boxers openly displaying their banners, on which was the following inscription: "Exterminate the foreigners and save the dynasty."

Covering a period of over four months, the foreign ministers at Peking made representation after representation to the Chinese government seeking a cessation of the Boxer movement, but to no avail. By this time (May), the whole

(China)

city of Peking was in a state of turmoil - murder and pillage were of daily occurrence. The reactionary prince, Tuan, and the Manchus generally, together with the Kan-suh soldiery under the notorious Tung-fu-hsiang, openly sided with the Boxers. The European residents and a large number of native converts took refuge in the British legation. On the 11th of June the chancellor of the Japanese legation was murdered by Chinese soldiers, while two days later most of the foreign buildings, churches and mission houses in the eastern part of the Tartar City were pillaged and burnt, and hundreds of native Chinese converts were massacred. As if this was insufficient to satisfy their hatred for everything foreign, they perpetrated and carried out still another horrible crime on the 20th - that of the unprovoked murder of Baron von Ketteler, German Minister, whilst on his way to the Tsung-Li-Yamen; a little later in the same day Chinese troops opened fire upon the Legation.

Cables and telegraph lines were choked with messages beseeching assistance for the defense of the foreign legation. However, this means of communication was soon ended, as well as all other methods, by the action of the Boxers in severing all lines of communication leading in to Peking. A small force of Marines and bluejackets, among which were twenty-seven American Marines, under Captain Newt H. Hall from the Oregon, and 25 others from the Newark, under Captain John T. Myers, who had been landed at Taku on the 24th and 28th of May, respectively, together with those of various other nationalities had reached the city before the Boxers had encircled it with troops, but this force was so insignificant compared to that which the Boxers now mustered, that the effective defense of the legations could not long be expected.

Vice Admiral Sir Edward H. Seymour, of the British Navy, headed a force consisting of 112 American Marines and sailors, under the command of Captain B. H. McCalla, U.S.N., together with Austrian, British, French, German, Italian and Japanese marines and sailors and proceeded on June 5 to the relief of the foreign legations in Peking. However, on the 19th, after having suffered severe losses, this combined force was compelled to abandon the expedition and return to Tientsin. On the 22nd, during the retreat, this force met stubborn resistance about eight miles outside of the city of Tientsin proper. Their progress had been checked by a strong Chinese Boxer force which was in position in the Siku Arsenal. The force under Admiral Seymour attacked this position with vigor and much bravery and after a few hours fighting his force was enabled to dislodge the Boxer force and take possession of the Arsenal themselves. The

(China)

reinforced Boxer forces however, invested the Arsenal and held the relief column beleaguered until they were relieved by reinforcements from other sources.

In the meantime, the American government was by no means idle. The nearest American forces which could be drawn upon to furnish reinforcements, were those stationed in the Philippines, consisting of Marines and army troops. Rear Admiral George C. Reamey was in command of the Asiatic Station, and he was directed to furnish all possible assistance to the beleaguered legations in Peking. He, in turn, ordered all available Marines from Manila and Olongapo to be despatched to Taku in preparation for the march on Peking. Major Littleton W. T. Waller, with 7 other officers, together with 131 Marines sailed from the Philippines on the Newark, on the 14th of June, arriving at Taku four days later. The commanding general of the United States army forces, also despatched several companies of the 9th and 14th Infantry, and Reilley's battery of artillery, under command of Brigadier General Adna R. Chaffee, but these troops did not reach China until some time after the Marines had arrived.

Upon arrival at Taku, Major Waller immediately landed his force, and started the march to Tong-ku, some 13 miles distant. At this latter place was the terminus of a railway to the interior, but the track was torn up in numerous places, and the rolling stock had been deserted. After surmounting many difficulties, repairs were finally made to the track and rolling stock, and a train prepared for the transportation of the Marines toward Tientsin.

While on the march from Taku to Tong-ku, Major Waller and his force overtook a battalion of Russian infantry, consisting of approximately 450 officers and men, who joined his force, and in company marched on to Tong-ku. They also accompanied the American Marines on the train towards Tientsin. This combined force arrived at a point about 12 miles from Tientsin at about 11 o'clock on the night of June 20th, where they went into bivouac. It was Major Waller's intention to wait here until reinforcements should arrive — believing his own force together with the Russians, was much too small to begin active operations. However, the Russian commander appeared so anxious to begin the forward march that Major Waller finally yielded, and joined the advance.

Early on the morning of the 21st the combined force started the advance and, by half after six, had reached a point opposite the imperial arsenal, when the enemy opened fire. Lightly at first, but presently heavily, and with considerable accuracy. The Americans and Russians, being

(China)

outnumbered more than two to one, were forced to retreat after two hours of sanguinary fighting - the American Marines suffering 3 killed and 7 wounded. The Marines, during the retreat, took up the dangerous position of rear guard, and successfully fought off all pursuers. About the middle of the afternoon the force reached their original base, 12 miles distant from Tientsin, where they awaited reinforcements. Major Waller's estimate of the situation had been proved correct.

Reinforcements arrived during the night of the 22nd, and consisted of additional Russian soldiers, an English force, German, Italian and Japanese - the total of all arms approximating 2000 officers and men. The commanders of the allied troops now held a conference, which ended by an agreement to again take up the advance early in the morning of the 24th, advancing in two columns. This plan was carried out, and by 4 o'clock, the columns encountered stiff resistance, but forced their way into the city about noon. By this time Major Waller's Marines had suffered 4 killed and 11 wounded. The whole allied force now rested for the remainder of the day. The respite was short, because soon after midnight of the 25th, they moved on to the relief of the beleaguered force under Vice-Admiral Seymour, who, it will be remembered was invested in Siku arsenal. This mission having been accomplished, the whole force moved back to Tientsin early in the morning of the 28th.

The Russians made an attack on the arsenal the 27th - the one where Major Waller was repulsed on the 21st - but were forced to call for reinforcements. Major Waller sent 1 officer and 40 of his Marines to their assistance, but placed them under the direct command of Commander Craddock, British Navy. And with this added force, the Boxers were driven out, the fortification captured, and the enemy put to flight. Major Waller, in closing his report of the operations, makes this rather pessimistic statement: "There seems small chance of any movement toward Peking for three weeks." No doubt he had reference to what he believed an inadequate force, and to the lack of cooperation on the part of the different commanders, with special reference to the Russian commander, General Stessel, who styled himself, "General commanding allied forces."

Major Waller predicted that should a considerable delay ensue before the advance on Peking be taken up, the Boxers would bring in reinforcements which would prevent, or at least deter an early march to the relief of the legations. Again his estimate of the situation was correct, because

(China)

the Chinese did send reinforcements to the number of some 10,000 officers and men, under the command of General Ma San Yuan, while some of the allied commanders were trying to bring about a unity of action of all. The British, Japanese and the Americans were in accord as to the necessity of quick action, but the others, particularly General Stessel, would not lend their cooperation for such a move.

The net result of this lack of cooperation was, as previously stated, the advent on the scene of a large force of Chinese troops, which must be defeated before an advance by the Relief Expedition was possible. It was not until July 8th that the commanders, less General Stessel, who maintained a status quo, finally came to an agreement, and a plan adopted for the continuance of the advance. This was ordered for the following morning, the 9th, and was carried out. The American Marines carried their part of the line, captured the arsenal, and there maintained themselves though outnumbered by about ten to one. The Russians were not permitted to remain idle for long, however, for the other forces drove the Boxers in their direction, when they were compelled to take an active part for their own safety. A result of this inactivity on the part of the Russians early in the attack, was the causing of the whole force to consolidate their position when they might have pushed on and defeated the enemy with assistance of the Russian troops.

Nothing could be done now excepting to hold the positions gained and wait for additional allied troops. These came on the 13th in the way of United States Marines, under the command of Colonel Robert L. Meade, together with 17 other officers and 300 men. At a conference, held shortly after Colonel Meade's arrival, it was agreed to continue the attack the following morning, the 13th. Colonel Meade placed his own force and that of Major Waller under the direction of the British commander, Brigadier General A.R.F. Dorward, and they fought side by side of the English troops all day. At 8 o'clock that night General Dorward ordered the men to "sleep on their arms," and continue the attack on the 14th. This plan was carried out, and the Allied Relief Expedition entered the "Walled City" at 6 in the morning. After the city had been taken, General Dorward addressed a letter to the American commander, in which he complimented the Marines in the highest terms.

Shortly after the fall of Tientsin, Colonel Meade was relieved and ordered to other duty. His detachment left the Marines again under the command of Major Waller. How-

(China) 38

ever, on August 3rd, Major William P. Biddle arrived with additional Marines and, being senior, relieved Major Waller. This new force of Marines brought their total to 482 officers and men. The following day, the 4th, the long delayed march on Peking commenced. During this long trek, lasting ten days, only two contacts of note were had with the enemy - the first at Pietsang on the 5th, and the second at Yangtsun the 6th. The American Marines did not take part in the first, but in the second, the Marines, the 9th and 14th Infantry units and Reilley's battery of the 5th Artillery, were all engaged. This attack was of short duration, and the Allied column continued its advance.

The Allied force arrived before the gates of Peking on the 14th of August, and on the next day the Imperial City was attacked and later captured - the United States Marines leading the attacking force. They took a position over the Chien-men gate, and cleared the barricades to permit the artillery to fire on the pagoda. Shortly after, two companies of the Marine force were posted in the pagoda, while the 2nd Battalion took up a position along the wall, from which they opened a heavy rifle fire on the Chinese troops in the Imperial City. The Chinese resisted stubbornly, but were finally driven out, leaving the Marines in complete possession of the gate. On the 16th they captured the west gate - holding both until the 19th, when they moved into the Tartar City.

During the fighting of the 15th, Captain David D. Porter (of the famous Porters of the Navy), together with First Lieutenant Leor M. Harding, captured several Chinese flags in a most gallant manner.

While the Allied force was engaged in reducing the fortifications of Tientsin, relieving the beleaguered force under Admiral Seymour, and making its march on Peking, the United States Marines from the Newark and Oregon (mentioned previously), were experiencing their own troubles in an endeavor to hold off the Boxers until help should arrive. Their experiences and activities probably can best be told by using the words of the American Minister himself, Honorable Edwin H. Conger, as contained in his official report to the Secretary of State: "To our Marines fell the most difficult and dangerous portion of the defense by reason of our proximity to the great wall and the main city gate, over which the large guns were planted. Our legation, with the position which we held on the wall, was the key to the whole

(China)

situation. This given up, all, including many Chinese Christians, would at once be driven into the British legation, and the congestion there increased by several hundred. The United States Marines acquitted themselves nobly. Twice were they driven from the wall, and once forced to abandon the legation, but each time, reinforced, immediately retook it, and with only a handful of men, aided by ten Russian sailors, and for a few days a few British marines, held it to the last against several hundred Chinese, with at least three pieces of artillery. The bravest and most successful event of the whole seige was an attack led by Captain Myers, of our Marines, and 55 men - American, British and Russian - which resulted in the capture of a formidable barricade on the wall, defended by several hundred Chinese soldiers, over 50 of whom were killed. Two United States Marines were killed and Captain Myers and a British Marine wounded. This made our position on the wall secure, and it was held to the last with the loss of only one other man. * * * I cannot close this dispatch without gratefully mentioning the splendid service performed by the United States Marines, who arrived here on May 31, under the command of Captain Myers. * * * Their conduct won the admiration and gratitude of all, and I beg you to kindly communicate the facts to the Navy Department."

The United States Marines remained in Peking until September 28th, when they were ordered back to the Philippine Islands. At the same time, all of the United States Army units were likewise withdrawn, except the Legation guard which, contrary to custom, was composed entirely of army troops instead of Marines.

(1905)

It was previously mentioned that a company of the 9th United States Infantry was retained as a guard for the American Legation at Peking, China, after that city was captured by the Allied Relief Column in August, 1900, and which was contrary to the usual custom. During the fore part of this year considerable correspondence passed between the Departments of State, War and Navy, the American Minister, Marine Corps Headquarters, and the Executive Office of President "Teddy" Roosevelt, relative to substituting the Marines for the Army unit at the Legation. The final result of these communications was an order signed by direction of the President, on the 31st of July, directing that the United States Marines relieve the 9th Infantry unit as guard at the American Legation in Peking.

(China)

This order was transmitted to the Commandant of the Marine Corps, Brigadier General Commandant George F. Elliott, who, in turn, instructed the commanding officer of the 1st Brigade of Marines, stationed in the Philippines, to detail 2 officers and 100 picked men, and transfer them to Peking. In accordance with this direction, Captain Harry Lee, First Lieutenant Thomas Holcomb, Jr., and 100 men were selected, embarked aboard the army transport Logan, proceeded to China and relieved the U.S. Army unit on the 12th of September. Beginning with this date, and continuing until the present, (1934), the United States Marines have maintained the American Legation Guard in Peking.

(1911)

The reform movement which began soon after the Chinese-Japanese War, continued to a more or less extent to the present, and as a result internal affairs remained in an unsettled state. Frequent uprisings occurred, and marauding bands roamed at will. Foreigners were molested, property damaged, and not a few kidnappings were perpetrated. As usual the United States kept naval vessels in Chinese waters to render assistance to Americans when such became necessary.

On the 4th of November two of these ships, the Albany, under the command of Commander R. H. Jackson, and the Rainbow, under Lieutenant Commander A. N. Mitchell, were at Shanghai looking after American interests. On the morning of this date a Chinese officer, General T'set Sun, went aboard the first named vessel, reporting that the revolutionary forces were in command of the river. In view of this condition, the two cable companies' property (Great Northern and Commercial), was in danger of being damaged. The Albany was moored to the dock, and the Rainbow was anchored in the stream, when, in consequence of the bad situation ashore, the latter ship sent 24 Marines to the former, to be used as guards if required. Commander Jackson, believing such action necessary, despatched 12 Marines to each of the cable stations on the evening of the 4th. They remained on this duty until the 14th, when they were withdrawn, and returned to the Rainbow.

(1912)

The revolution for the overthrow of the Manchu dynasty, which had its inception in the previous year, as well as a continuance of the reform movement, kept internal affairs in a constant state of upheaval. Rear Admiral Reginald F. Nicholson, who had relieved Admiral Murdock in July of this year, was keeping a close watch over affairs, and taking every precaution for the safety of Americans and American interests. On the 24th of August he ordered one company of Marines from the Rainbow, under command of Captain Thomas C. Turner, to be landed on Kentucky Island. They remained ashore for two days, when they were withdrawn. Another force was landed on the 26th at Camp Nicholson, and remained until the 30th, when it too, was withdrawn.

(1913)

During this year, especially around Shanghai, the revolutionary troops were quite active. The Albany, under the command of Commander Mark L. Bristol, and the Rainbow, under the command of Lieutenant Commander D.W. Wurtzbaugh, were at anchor at Shanghai at the time when, on July 7th, Commander Bristol deemed it necessary to land a force of Marines to protect the interests of the United States, but was withdrawn the same day. On the 28th of the same month it again became necessary to land Marines for the protection of American interests. The Albany landed a force in the evening of this date, as did also the Rainbow, under the command of Lieutenant-Commander Wurtzbaugh. These forces were withdrawn on the morning of the 29th, but they were again landed the same evening, and remained until the 14th and 17th of August, respectively.

(1922)

Internal political affairs in China had not resolved themselves into a tranquil state during the years since the last landing by United States Marines. In fact, during this year conditions grew worse, which caused the Legation Guard to be strengthened, and other landings as well. Commander Louis C. Richardson, of the Albany, received instructions the latter part of April to land his Marine detachment, under the command of Captain Charles H. Martin, as a reinforcement for the Legation at Peking. They landed on the 28th, and remained until the 25th of May, when they were withdrawn. A battalion of Marines, under the command of Captain Roy C. Swink, served for a time aboard the Huron, were landed at Taku on the 5th of May, and proceeded to Shanghai, where they remained until the 11th.

(China)

(1924)

The revolutionary movement was still in progress during this year, and because of the danger to United States citizens, their property, and American interests, it was found advisable to land Marines on several different occasions. The first landing took place on the 6th of October at Shanghai. On this date the Marine detachment of the Asheville (31 men), under First Lieutenant John T. Thornton, and the 1st Expeditionary Force (101 men), under Captain Francis S. Kieren, were landed due to the unsettled conditions at that place. The Asheville's detachment was withdrawn on the 24th, but the other force remained ashore. On the 31st of October the 1st Expeditionary Force proceeded from Shanghai to Tientsin, landed there on the 4th of November, where they continued on duty for the remainder of the year.

(1925)

The first of this year found the 1st Expeditionary Force still ashore at Tientsin. They remained there until the 8th of February, when they were withdrawn to the Asheville. On the 15th of January, the Marine detachment of the Sacramento (28 men), under First Lieutenant Howard N. Stent, was landed at Shanghai, and remained on shore until the 22nd. About the middle of January a Second Expeditionary Force was organized in the Philippines, under command of Captain James P. Schwerin, proceeded to Shanghai on the Barker, Borie and Whipple, landed at Shanghai on the 22nd of January, and remained there until the 9th of February, when they were withdrawn and returned to the Philippines. In the first part of June the 2nd Provisional Company (127 men), under Captain Angus Wilson, sailed from the Philippines, and landed at Shanghai on the 9th; remaining there until the 29th of August, when they were withdrawn to the Abarenda. They remained on this vessel until the 9th of November, when they landed at Tientsin, and the last of this year found them still there. On the 1st of July the Marine detachment of the Huron, under the command of Captain William P. Richards, was landed at Shanghai, where they remained until the 29th, when withdrawn. Still another detachment of 69 men, under Captain Omar T. Pfeiffer, landed at Shanghai on the 30th of December.

(1926)

The beginning of this year found the 2nd Provisional Company, and the detachment last mentioned above, at Tientsin and Shanghai, respectively. The first mentioned was

(China)

withdrawn to the Sacramento on the 9th of June, and the latter to the Pecos on the 12th of March.

In the latter part of this year the fighting between the different factions increased to such an extent that Rear Admiral Clarence S. Williams, commanding the Asiatic Fleet, deemed it necessary to despatch a considerable force to the scene of most danger which, at the time, appeared to be Chingwangtao. He ordered two officers, Captains Walter E. McCaughtry and Carl F. Herz, and 125 enlisted Marines from Guam to be embarked on the Gold Star, and sail without delay. They sailed on the 7th of November, and landed at Chingwangtao on the 12th.

(1927-1934)

The force last mentioned was augmented by the addition of the Expeditionary Battalion, consisting of the 88th, 89th, 90th and 91st Companies, under the command of Major Samuel P. Budd, who embarked aboard the Pecos at Cavite, proceeded to Shanghai, and landed there on the 9th of February, to assist in guarding the International Settlement. While this battalion was being organized and despatched to China, Admiral Williams had requested additional forces from the United States. The 4th Regiment of Marines was at San Diego, and it was quickly put in condition for service overseas. The Regiment, less the 2nd Battalion, under the command of Colonel Charles S. Hill, was embarked aboard the Chaumont, sailed on the 3rd of February, arrived on the 24th, but did not land to remain ashore until the 16th of March.

Captain George W. Steele, Jr., in the Pittsburgh, arrived at Shanghai about the middle of January, and on the 4th of March was ordered to send a landing force to retake the Meifoo XIV, a Standard Oil Company's vessel which had been commandeered by Chinese troops in the vicinity of Hangchow on the 19th of the previous month. Captain Steele detailed Lieutenant-Commander W.A. Edwards, two squads of Marines and two squads of bluejackets, who proceeded immediately and regained custody of the ship, returning it to the Standard Oil Company.

On the 25th of March, Captain Harold S. Fassett, Second Lieutenant Edwin C. Ferguson and 63 Marines landed at Shanghai to act as a patrol for the Bund. They returned aboard shortly before noon the following day. Again on the 31st the Marines were landed, and remained ashore until the 3rd of April. About the same time, Commander Irving H. Mayfield, in the Sacramento, was also at Shanghai, and on the 24th of March sent First Lieutenant John M. Greer and 16 of

(China)

his Marines ashore at Pootung to guard the property of the Universal Leaf and Tobacco Company. This detachment returned on the 19th of April.

On March 6th, Brigadier General Smedley D. Butler, with several staff officers, left San Francisco for the Orient, where, upon his arrival, he took over command of all United States Marine units then on shore. On the 26th of this same month, Admiral Williams again requested more Marines, as the forces then present would be incapable of handling a serious situation. In compliance with this last request, the 6th Regiment, less the 3rd Battalion, the 3rd Brigade Headquarters and Headquarters Company, 3rd Brigade Service Company, one battery of 75-mm. tractor-drawn artillery, and one squadron of scouting, pursuit and amphibian planes, the whole under the command of Colonel Harold C. Snyder, were sent from San Diego to Shanghai on the 7th of April on board the Henderson, arriving there on the 2nd of May. Before these last reinforcements had reached China, the 2nd Battalion of the 4th, and the 3rd Battalion of the 6th Regiments, together with the 1st Battalion of the 10th (artillery) Regiment, less one battery, one light tank platoon, the 5th Company of engineers (Marines), and the remainder of the 3rd Brigade aviation force, were despatched to the Philippines on the Dollar Line Steamer President Grant, where they arrived on the 4th of May, at Olongapo. Soon after these units arrived, they were formed into a provisional regiment. On the 11th of April the Guam aviation detachment sailed, arriving at Shanghai on the 25th.

About the middle of May, the 1st Battalion of the 10th Regiment, the 5th Company of Engineers, and the light tank platoon, was despatched from Olongapo to Shanghai to reinforce the 6th Regiment, arriving there on the 31st. About this time Tientsin resolved itself into a danger area for all foreigners, and the 6th Regiment, less the 3rd Battalion, under Colonel Snyder, the 1st Battalion of the 10th Regiment, under Colonel ~~XXXXXXXXXXXXXXXX~~ [Harry Lay], one light tank platoon and the 5th (engineer) Company, less one platoon, sailed from Shanghai for Taku on the 2nd of June, for further transfer to Tientsin, where they arrived on the 6th. General Butler proceeded to Tientsin and took command at that place, leaving the 4th Regiment at Shanghai.

Since the arrival in China of the units above mentioned, United States Marines have continued on duty in that country up to the time of this writing - August 31st, 1934 - although their strength has been materially reduced, the Fourth Regiment alone having been stationed in China since the 24th of January, 1929.

(China)

References: Cooper's Hist. Navy, III, 102; Collum's Hist. U.S. Marine Corps, 106-108; Sec. Navy An. Rep., 1894, 24; id., 1895, 526-528; id., 1898, II, 42; id., 1899, 922; id., 1900, 3-6, 448-450, 1116-1133; id., 1905, 1233-1234; id., 1912, 14,590; id., 1922, 822; Marine Corps Archives; St. Dept. Archives; Navy Archives; Major-General Commandant An. Rep., 1927, 9; Logs of Portsmouth, Powhatan, Plymouth, Levant, San Jacinto, Mississippi, Wachusett, Baltimore, Newark, Oregon, Albany, Huron, Rainbow, Asheville, Sacramento and Pittsburgh.

COLOMBIA

(1860)

For many years Colombia had endeavored to throw off the Spanish yoke. Revolution followed revolution, but none seemed to gain the desired end, until the advent of Bolivar in the year of 1819, when he accomplished his most striking achievement by suddenly crossing the inundated llanos, the Andes, fell upon the advance guards of the royalists, effected a union with Santander, routed the Spaniards at Boyaca on August 7th, marched into Bogota three days later, and assured the independence of New Granada.

The United States was the first foreign government to recognize the independence of Colombia, and comparative tranquility reigned until about 1858, when unrest and rumblings of revolutionary tenor began among the different factions of the populace. These manifestations later grew into open hostilities and, by 1860, a well defined revolution was in progress.

Commander William D. Porter, of the sloop St. Mary's was in the vicinity, and received instructions to proceed to the bay of Panama to observe conditions and to take whatever action he deemed necessary for the protection of American interests. He arrived on July 4th, but as conditions appeared to be tranquil, a landing was not made at the time. He remained, however, to await further developments. This delay proved opportune, for in the latter part of September conditions so changed that the landing of an armed force became necessary. On the 27th the Marine Guard, under Second Lieutenant Calvin L. Sayre, was despatched ashore to protect the railroad, and other American interests, from attacks of the insurrectionary forces. On the 29th an additional force of 50 sailors, under Lieutenant Thomas McK. Buchanan, was sent ashore to augment the Marines. Both the Marines and sailors remained until the 8th of October, when they returned to their ship.

(1873)

During the first part of this year hostilities again broke out over the possession of the government of the

(Colombia)

State of Panama. Rear Admiral Charles Steedman, U.S. Navy, commander-in-chief of the South Pacific squadron, with his flagship Pensacola and the Tuscarora, arrived in the bay of Panama on May 7th. Upon the request of the American Consul O. M. Long, together with requests of a number of influential Americans and other foreign residents he despatched ashore a force of 44 Marines, under First Lieutenant Henry J. Bishop, and about 160 sailors, with four pieces of artillery, the whole under the command of Lieutenant-Commander Theodore F. Jewell, of the Tuscarora, for the protection of the Consulate, American citizens and the railroad. This trouble soon subsided however, and the force from the Tuscarora was withdrawn on the 12th, while those of the flagship returned aboard three days later.

In the early part of September the lives and property of foreigners were again jeopardized because of a renewal of hostilities between the different factions from the same causes as had previously existed. Captain Albert G. Clary, commanding the Benicia, was the first to arrive at Panama; he was soon followed by Admiral Steedman, in the Pensacola. The latter arrived on the 18th, and consulted with the American Consul, who apparently thought the conditions warranted the landing of an armed force.

On the 22nd Admiral Steedman turned over his command to Rear Admiral John J. Almy, acquainted the latter with the local conditions, and then took his departure. The following day, 23rd, Admiral Almy ordered a landing force of 100 Marines and Sailors, with two howitzers, under the command of Captain Aaron K. Hughes to proceed ashore for the protection of lives and property of foreigners. The Marines were under the command of Captain Percival C. Pope, and Second Lieutenant James V. D'Hervilly of the Pensacola, and Second Lieutenant Henry G. Ellsworth of the Benicia. Additional officers and men were sent ashore on the 24th, 25th, 26th, 27th and 28th as reinforcements for the troops first landed. On October 1st Captain Clement D. Hebb,

(Colombia)

U.S. Marine Corps, reported aboard the Pensacola for duty, and the same day, President Niera of the State of Panama, accompanied by the American Consul visited Admiral Almy aboard the latter's vessel. On the 4th (October), the Marines and sailors ashore from the Benicia, returned on board that vessel, and those from the Pensacola, returned on the 9th. Admiral Almy remained in the harbor until the 24th, while the Benicia did not take her departure until December 14th.

(1885)

Conditions in the Isthmus remained quiet for about twelve years, but at the end of that time a recurrence of the same trouble manifested itself in the form of another revolution. This time the danger to foreign interests was on the Atlantic side, at Aspinwall (now Colon). Commander Lewis Clark, in the Alliance, arrived at this place on the 16th of January, and the following morning received a visit from the American Consul Robert K. Wright, Jr., who reported the conditions to Commander Clark, and requested that a Marine guard be sent ashore to protect the Panama Railroad Company's property. The Marine Guard of this vessel was under the command of First Lieutenant Louis J. Gulick, and the Commander instructed him to select a suitable number of men and proceed ashore on the duty in question. The Marines were landed on the 18th, and withdrawn the following day.

Less than two months had elapsed before conditions on the Isthmus necessitated the sending of other American warships to this land of seemingly perpetual revolution for the protection of United States interests. Commander Theodore F. Kane, in the Galena, was the first to reach Aspinwall, where he arrived on the 11th of March. He consulted with the American Consul, Mr. Wright, and on the 16th detailed Second Lieutenant Charles A. Doyen and 16 of his Marines as a landing party for the protection of American interests, due to the fact that the Colombian Government had left the city without proper forces to make sure the safety of foreigners. A little later the same day 1 officer and 12 additional men were sent on shore, and on the 17th and 19th still more officers and men were likewise despatched.

(Colombia)

An incident took place on March 30th, which, but for prompt action might have had serious consequences. The American steamer Colon was moored alongside her wharf, and at 1:40 p.m. her Ensign was discovered to be hoisted at the fore, Union down. Commander Kane despatched Lieutenant Charles Judd to learn the nature of her difficulties, and he returned shortly with the information that the Colon had arms and ammunition aboard, and that Prestan (a Haitian negro and one of the chiefs of the insurgents) demanded their delivery to him, but the captain of the steamer would not consent.

Upon receipt of this report Commander Kane then despatched Lieutenant Judd, accompanied by Naval Cadet Richardson, to communicate with the agents of the Pacific Mail Steamship Company, Mr. Dow and Mr. Connor, relative to the munitions aboard the Colon. Cadet Richardson returned in about 45 minutes with the startling information that Prestan had arrested Lieutenant Judd, Consul Wright, Mr. Dow and Connor, and intended to hold them in prison until the arms and ammunition were delivered to him, and lastly, should any force from the Galena attempt to land they would be fired upon, or should the Galena herself fire, all of the prisoners would be immediately shot. This was an ultimatum that no American officer had ever suffered himself to accept, and Commander Kane being no exception, ordered his starboard battery loaded with grape, and trained on the insurgents collecting on the Pier and Dock of the steamship company. This act had the desired effect, for in less than an hour Lieutenant Judd returned, and stated that the other prisoners had likewise been released, so ending the incident.

Commander Kane next moved his vessel as close to the Colon as practicable, and sent a detail aboard to take her out into the stream. This accomplished, he then sent a boat for the Consul, the agents of the steamship company, and the general superintendent of the Panama Railroad, Mr. Burt, to bring them aboard for safety. The agents, however, could not be located.

(Colombia)

The following day (March 31st), a battalion consisting of Lieutenant Doyen and 18 of his Marines, together with naval officers and sailors to the strength of 126, were sent on shore to guard American property, and were stationed at the Consulate, office of the Pacific Mail Company and the Panama Railroad offices. Shortly after this force went ashore, Colombian troops arrived, and engaged the Insurgents, who were compelled to withdraw into the city. About mid-day a fire broke out in the city near the barricades behind which the Insurgents had taken up their position, and it was not long before it was sweeping everything before it; even the docks were consumed by the flames. The battalion on shore assisted in fighting the fire, and in preventing pillage of the shops, houses, etc.

During the fighting and conflagration on shore, about 300 refugees were cared for on board the Galena. The majority of these were returned ashore on April 2nd, and the Panama Railroad furnished them with free transportation to Panama City. On this date two Insurgents, Antonio Pautrizelle and George Davis, both negroes, were among those who sought safety on the American man-of-war. These two men remained aboard until May 6th, when they were sent ashore under a guard of Marines, and turned over to General Reyes of the Colombian forces, who ordered them executed by hanging the same day.

The Alliance returned to Aspinwall on April 8th, and the Tennessee, with Rear Admiral James E. Jouett aboard, arrived on the 10th. Prior to this the Navy Department had ordered an expeditionary force made ready for immediate duty on the Isthmus, consisting of Marines and seamen, and this force proceeded thereto on the steamships City of Para and Acapulco, on April 3rd and 7th, respectively. The Marines, under Major Charles Heywood, sailed on the former vessel and arrived at Aspinwall on the 10th. On the 11th Major Heywood and his battalion of Marines were despatched to Panama City (where General Aizpuru of the

(Colombia)

Insurgents had retired after his defeat at Aspinwall), for the protection of United States interests, and to reinforce the American forces which had been landed from the Shenandoah. On the 8th of April this ship had landed her Marine Guard, under first Lieutenant Thomas N. Wood, 9 naval officers, an artillery company and 2 infantry companies of sailors, the whole under the direct command of Lieutenant-Commander Edwin Longnecker. This battalion, less the Marines and the artillery company, returned to the ship on the 13th, and on the 17th the Marines returned, but were landed again three days later to form a part of the force under Major Heywood. This duty was continued until the 30th, when the entire force from the Shenandoah returned to the ship.

Upon the arrival of the Acapulco, on April 15th, Commander B. H. McCalla was ordered to assume command of all forces ashore, and as the Expeditionary Force was considered to be of sufficient strength to cope with conditions on shore, detachments from the squadron were relieved and returned to their ships. On the 21st the headquarters were moved to Panama, due to the fact that the Insurgents had transferred their activities to that place, and it was feared they would destroy this city as they had Aspinwall. Conditions became so grave that, on the 24th, Commander McCalla called for the garrison stationed at Aspinwall, and the reserve battalion of Marines from the ships of the squadron. Upon the arrival of this additional force, the city was occupied, Aizpuru and his leaders were arrested, and detained until a stipulation was signed that fighting should not take place within the limits of the town. This stipulation was signed the following day, and the American forces were withdrawn to a position at the railroad depot.

Colonels Montoya and Reyes of the Colombian forces arrived on the 28th. The following day a conference took place between them, the chief of the Insurgents Aizpuru, and Rear Admiral Jouett, which resulted in the capitulation of the insurgent troops. This re-establishment of national authority rendered the presence of the American expeditionary force no longer necessary, and the greater part of it was withdrawn on May 16th and by the 25th the remainder was withdrawn and the entire force returned to the United States.

(1895)

Again, in the early part of this year, unrest and

(Colombia)

revolutionary tendencies manifested themselves on the Isthmus of Panama. Due to this almost continuous state of insurrectionary disturbances, the United States kept men-of-war vessels in the adjacent waters, and within easy sailing distance of the Isthmus should their services be required for the protection of American interests. On March 7th, Captain Bartlett J. Cromwell, aboard the cruiser Atlanta, anchored in the harbor of Bocas del Toro, for the purpose of observing conditions, as fighting was in progress between government troops and some insurgent forces.

The following morning Captain Cromwell received a request to furnish an armed landing force for the protection of American lives and property. He granted this request, and selected a "Sergeant's Guard of Marines," together with a company of Bluejackets and a Gatling gun, under the command of Commander Edward D. Taussig, and despatched them ashore with instructions to protect the lives and property of foreigners. This uprising soon quieted, and the landing force was withdrawn the following day, the 9th, but the Atlanta remained in the vicinity for more than a month before leaving for other waters.

(1901)

Slightly over six years had elapsed since the last landing by American armed forces on the Isthmus before their presence was again required because of a new revolution, - or should one say: a new outbreak, of a continued revolution, occurred in this troubled area. Apparently Panama was determined to gain its independence regardless of the number of years it took or the number of revolutions necessary to gain that objective.

In the latter part of this year the Liberal and National troops were engaged in a fierce struggle for the supremacy of authority, in the matter of establishing the State of Panama as a separate republic. This conflict endangered the lives and property of all foreign residents. Great Britain and France despatched naval vessels to the area for the protection of their nationals. The United States also sent several vessels of the navy to the Isthmus for the same purpose. British interests were represented by H.M.S. Tribune, while those of France were in care of the Suchet. The interests of the United States were entrusted to the Iowa, Captain Thomas Perry; Concord, Com-

(Colombia)

mander Gottfried Blocklinger; *Marietta*, Commander Francis H. Delano, and the *Machias*, Lieutenant Commander Nathan Sargent.

The British and French ships were at Aspinwall (Colon), as were also two of the American vessels, the *Machias* and *Marietta*, while the *Concord* and *Iowa* were on the opposite side, at Panama. The *Marietta* and *Concord* arrived on November 23rd, having been preceded by over a month by the other two ships. Captain Perry having consulted with the American Consul, Hezekiah A. Gudger, and other officials, concluded that a landing force was necessary to protect the interests of his Government. He therefore directed a battalion of Marines and seamen made ready and, at 3:40 p.m. the 24th, they left the ship and proceeded on this duty. The Marines of the *Iowa* were under the command of Captain Albert S. McLemore, with Second Lieutenant Edward A. Greene as second in command, while those of the other ships were in charge of noncommissioned officers. On the 25th the *Concord* also sent a battalion of Marines and seamen ashore, and both forces remained on this service until December 4th, when they were withdrawn.

While these landings were taking place at Panama, other landings were being made at Aspinwall (Colon), from the *Machias* and *Marietta*. These forces landed on the 26th, and their composition - Marines and sailors - was the same as the force landed at Panama. Captain Perry, after despatching the landing forces ashore at Panama, proceeded to Aspinwall and, on the 28th of November, held a conference aboard the *Marietta*, which was attended by the commanding officers of the English and French vessels, General Alban of the Colombian troops, and General de la Rosa of the Liberal army. At this conference it was agreed that the Liberal forces should demoblize, turn their arms over to the foreign naval authorities then present, and the city relinquished to General Alban's control. The transfer of authority took place the following day at 2:00 p.m. in the afternoon, and was accompanied by appropriate ceremonies.

During the time that the American landing forces were ashore, they furnished guards of Marines for all trains of the Panama Railroad crossing the Isthmus, the last guard being withdrawn at (by) 10:00 a.m. the 4th of December.

(Colombia)

(1902)

The cessation of hostilities, brought about by Captain Perry in the previous November, was of short duration. Hardly six months had passed before the Liberal and Government forces were again engaged in open warfare. Commander Henry McCrea, in the *Machias*, was ordered from Santo Domingo to the Isthmus of Panama, where he arrived on the 12th of April, at Aspinwall. Here Commander McCrea visited the American Consul, David R. Hand, and the same evening proceeded to Bocas del Toro, arriving there the following day. The Liberal forces were quite active in this vicinity, and Commander McCrea despatched several messages to the commander of these forces relative to the protection of American interests. An attack on the town being momentarily expected, which if carried out would endanger the lives and property of Americans, a guard of two officers and 28 men were landed on the 16th to furnish the necessary protection.

Early the following morning heavy firing was heard from shoreward, and that evening a boat was despatched ashore containing Surgeon F.M. Bogan and others, to assist in carrying wounded Colombian soldiers, within the lines established by the American landing force, and the dressing of their wounds. During the same afternoon the Liberal commander requested Commander McCrea to communicate with the Government leaders, and if practicable arrange a capitulation for the Liberal forces. About 7:30 that evening the leaders of the opposing forces repaired aboard the *Machias*, and together with Commander McCrea drew up the necessary agreement for the cessation of hostilities. Early the next morning, the 18th, the Marines and a company of sailors were sent ashore to be present at the surrender of the Liberal forces, which was done in accordance with the agreement signed the previous day, and the landing force, with the exception of the Marines, were withdrawn, the latter remaining until the 19th before returning to their ship.

About mid-afternoon on the 19th, the Colombian gunboat *Pinzon* and the transport *Marcellus*, arrived, and it appeared that they were loaded with Government troops, under the command of General Gomez. He was informed of the negotiations entered into by the Liberal and Government forces ashore, and warned of the necessity of giving the required notice before beginning a bombardment of the town. As General Gomez did not order the Government ships to leave

(Colombia)

the harbor, Commander McCrea deemed it advisable to send another force ashore as a precaution in case fighting should be renewed. Accordingly, a party of two officers and 28 men were again landed in the town shortly after noon of the 20th. About 5:00 p.m. the Colombian transport went alongside the dock, and disembarked her troops. The following morning, the 21st, the German steamer _Hercynia_ arrived with additional Colombian troops, and they were landed at Old Bank. At the request of General Gomez, Commander McCrea sent his Marine Guard ashore on the evening of the 21st to guard foreign interests during the evacuation of the Liberal forces. This guard returned aboard the following morning.

On the 23rd Commander McCrea sailed for Aspinwall, where he remained until May 16th, when he received cable orders to return to Bocas del Toro. He sailed immediately and arrived at the latter place about noon the 17th. However, this new difficulty was straightened out without the landing of another armed force, and the _Machias_, after cruising along the coast and stopping at different places, sailed for Cape Haitien on July 23rd. Before she sailed, however, Commander William P. Potter, in the _Ranger_, had arrived at Panama. Conditions in this city remained quiet until the middle of September, when it was necessary to send a landing party ashore for protection of foreigners. This party was first landed on the 18th, but withdrawn each night thereafter until the 23rd, when they were entirely withdrawn.

Conditions at Aspinwall were by no means tranquil. Commander Thomas C. McLean, in the _Cincinnati_, arrived at the latter place on the 15th of September. He found conditions such as to require the landing of an armed force to protect American interests. This force was landed on the 17th, and part of it was diverted to guard the trains crossing the Isthmus, while the remainder protected lives and property in the city. It returned aboard each night, however, and went ashore each morning until the 21st.

In the meantime the Navy Department had ordered the Commandant of the Marine Corps to furnish an expeditionary battalion of his Corps for service in Panama. This battalion, organized under orders of September 11th, consisted of 16 officers and 325 enlisted men, under the command of Lieutenant-Colonel Benjamin R. Russell, U.S.M.C., sailed on the _Panther_ the 14th, and arrived at Aspinwall

(Colombia)

(Colon) on the 22nd. The following day the battalion was landed, and went into camp where they remained until November 16th. On this date a part of the battalion was withdrawn, and on the 18th the entire force returned aboard the Panther.

References: Eder, Colombia, 31-35; Sec. Navy An. Rep., 1873, 8; id., 1885, XV-XVII; Major-General Commandant An. Rep., 1902, 992-993; St. Dept. Archives; Navy Archives; Marine Corps Archives; Logs of St. Mary's, Pensacola, Tuscarora, Benicia, Tennessee, Alliance, Galena, Atlanta, Ranger, Concord, Marietta, Machias, Cincinnati and Panther.

COREA

(1871)

For several years American sailors, and others, who were shipwrecked in the waters adjacent to the shores of Corea, and who had been able to reach land, had been most foully dealt with by the natives. Many had been murdered outright, and others heinously treated in various ways.

These conditions became so serious that in the spring of this year the American Minister to China, Mr. Frederick F. Low, was instructed to arrange a convention with the Corean authorities for the protection of American citizens. To carry out this mission, Mr. Low enlisted the services of the Asiatic Fleet, commanded by Rear Admiral John Rodgers, which was then in the harbor of Nagasaka, Japan. Accordingly, Mr. Low boarded Rodger's flagship, the Colorado, and the squadron sailed for Corean waters. It arrived off the Salee River anchorage on May 21st. After an exchange of visits on the part of the Coreans and Americans, the former seemed satisfied that the mission was peaceful and friendly. During these visits the Admiral obtained consent to send a surveying party up the river to make soundings for the safety of commerce and navigation. Such a party was accordingly sent upon this mission; had proceeded well above the forts, and were engaged in making soundings, when suddenly and treacherously they were fired upon from the forts and the shore. The small vessels which had accompanied the party, hurried into action, drove the Coreans from their works, and rescued the surveyors.

The American Minister and the Admiral decided that this outrage should be explained, and a demand made for reparation. This decision was carried out, the Corean authorities notified, and a ten day period given for them to make reply. This period having passed with no reply from the Coreans, the American officials planned an attack upon the forts and citadel from which the outrage had been committed.

On the 10th of June the Monocacy and Palos, with four steam-launches, carrying a landing party of one battalion of Marines, commanded by Captain McLane Tilton, a brigade of seamen infantry, and seven field pieces, all under the command of Captain Homer C. Blake of the Alaska, proceeded up the Salee River to engage the forts. This little flotilla had not been underway long before the forts opened fire. This fire was of short duration, for the guns of the Monocacy and Palos quickly silenced them. Captain Tilton with his Marines, who were in the steam-launches, were cast loose and landed -- followed immediately by the naval brigade. The landing was most difficult because of deep mud, scrub, and small arms firing from a redoubt on their right flank. As the Marines advanced, the garrison of the fort fled, firing as they went, but with no effect. The Marines entered the fort, spiked the guns, and proceeded with its dismantling while waiting for the seamen to come up. When this work was finished, evening was far advanced, and an order was issued for the entire force to bivouac on a wooded hill for the night. Incidentally, this was the first time in history that a Western force had spent the night on Corean soil.

The following morning, the 11th, an advance was made on the second line of fortifications. The Marines again led the way. One-third assaulted the face of the works, the others being held in support. However, the assault was a bloodless one; the enemy having decamped, and possession was had without firing a shot. The fort was speedily dismantled, and the attention of the force was turned towards the citadel, which had been the chief offender in the earlier outrage.

This citadel was built upon the apex of a conical hill, some 150 feet high from the bottom of the ravine, through which the Marines had to pass to reach the fortification. The hill was very steep, the walls of the fort joined the acclivity with scarcely a break in the line, and had not the guns of the Monocacy and the howitzers on shore, shattered the walls, it would have been almost impossible for the Marines to scale them. Nothing seemed to be able to check the Marines and sailors; they swarmed over the parapet to come to hand-to-hand blows with the defenders, who were unyielding – giving no quarter and expecting none – and only when the last man fell did the conflict cease. The remaining forts made no resistance; the garrisons fled, and the conflict was over with complete success to American arms. The enemy's yellow cotton flag, with its large Chinese cabalistic character in the center, which flew over the fort, was captured by Private Hugh Purvis and Corporal Charles Brown, of the Marine guards of the Colorado and Alaska.

Commander Kimberly, who commanded the shore operations, in his report of the affair, says: "To Captain Tilton and his Marines belong the honor of first landing and last leaving the shore, in leading the advance on the march, in entering the forts, and in acting as skirmishers. Chose as the advance guard, on account of their steadiness and discipline, and looked to with confidence in case of difficulty, their whole behaviour on the march and in the assault proved that it was not misplaced."

(Corea)

On the morning of the 12th (June), after having occupied the field of battle for eighteen hours; capturing 480 pieces of ordnance, 50 flags among which was the flag of the generalissimo, inflicting casualties upon the enemy of about 250 killed and many wounded, the whole force returned to their respective ships. The Marine casualties were two: Private Dennis Harrigan killed, and Private Michael Owen wounded.

(1888)

The Corean "pot" continued to "boil," with an occasional outbreak which threatened foreign consulates, and foreign citizens and their property. One of these occurred in June of this year at Seoul, the capital. The American Minister deemed it serious enough to warrant an armed force to protect the interests of the United States. The Essex, Commandant Theodore F. Jewell, commanding, was moored in the harbor of Chemulpo and the Minister requested him to furnish a suitable guard, which he did. At 8:55 p.m. on the 19th (June), a landing force of 12 Marines and 13 sailors, with 1st Lieutenant Robert D. Wainwright of the Marines, Ensign Hoggatt and Lieutenant C. D. Galloway of the Navy, commanding, left the ship, marched to Seoul (25 miles) and reported to the American Minister as guard for the Consulate. This force remained on this duty until the 30th, at which time they returned to their ship.

(1894)

The war between China and Japan, which began on July 25th of this year, was the occasion for unrest and disturbed conditions in this country. In June, Rear Admiral McNair, commander-in-chief, Asiatic Fleet, sent the Baltimore to Corea to observe conditions, and to be near in case the American Minister should request assistance. On the 22nd of July the Japanese troops seized the palace and the king. The following day (23rd), the American Minister requested Captain Day, of the Baltimore, to send a guard to protect the consulate, missionaries, and other foreign residents of Seoul. Accordingly, Captain Day ordered Captain George F. Elliott of the Marines, to take charge of a detachment of two ensigns, an assistant surgeon, a paymaster's clerk, 21 Marines and 29 sailors and proceed to Seoul. It was intended to send this force by boat. However, there being no pilot available, Captain Elliott suggested that he be permitted to march, which was agreed to by Captain Day. Captain Elliott with the 21 Marines, only, left the ship

(Corea)

at 7:30 p.m. the 24th, and made a night march to the capital. The naval contingent of this force proceeded up the river in boats the next day, and reported to Captain Elliott upon arrival. Elliott's force remained at Seoul until the 26th of September, when it was relieved by a detachment of 18 Marines from the Concord, under command of Lieutenant Gill of the Navy. This latter force remained until October 29th, when it was withdrawn. On the 2nd of November, the Marine Guard of the Charleston, under 1st Lieutenant B. S. Neumann, U.S.M.C., landed and took the place of the guard from the Concord.

(1895)

The beginning of this year found the Marines from the Charleston still on duty at the American legation. They remained on this duty until March 25th. The Marines from the Detroit relieved them at this time; remaining until the 19th of June, when they returned to their ship. The Legation had no guard from that date until October 11th, when the Yorktown landed her guard. This detachment was withdrawn on November 30th, having been relieved by the Marines of the Machias the day before.

(1896)

The Machias' Marines continued their duty as guard for the American legation during the early part of this year, and were not withdrawn until April 3rd.

(1904)

In December of the previous year a detachment of Marines, under Captain Arthur J. Matthews, U.S.M.C., consisting of 2 other officers and 100 men, sailed from the Philippine Islands on the Zafiro for Corea. This force landed on January 5th this year, proceeded to Seoul, and established a guard at the American Legation.

(1905)

The guard established the previous year was continued until November 11th of this year, when it was transferred back to the Philippine Islands, joining the 1st Regiment of Marines at that place.

References: Collum's Hist. U.S. Marine Corps, 202, 310-313; Memo Solic. St. Dept., 59, 61, 63-64; Sec. Navy An. Rep., 1871, 27; id., 1888, xx-xxi; id., 1894, 523; Logs of Monocacy and Palos; Hamersly Gen. Reg., 100 Yrs., 76; Marine Corps Archives; Marine Corps Muster Rolls, Essex;

(Corea)

Log of *Essex*, June '83; World's Alm., 751; Marine Corps Muster Rolls, *Baltimore* and *Concord*; Log of *Baltimore*, July 1894; Major-General Commandant An. Rep., 1904, 1188-1189; Marine Corps Chronology; Marine Corps Muster Rolls.

C U B A

(1906)

Before this little Island Republic was ten years old a revolution of considerable proportions was well underway. By the middle of this year its affairs were in a chaotic condition. The officials of the United States felt that there was a poor outlook for a change for the better, and that intervention was necessary to bring about order, protection to foreigners and the establishment of a stable regime to administer properly the affairs of government.

All preliminary steps having been completed, the Marine Headquarters was directed, on September 14th, to assemble three battalions of Marines for duty in the troubled area and, on the 25th of the same month, two additional battalions. The first three battalions sailed on the Tacoma, Newark and Minneapolis on September 16th, 17th and 18th, respectively. The additional two battalions sailed on the Prairie, Texas and Brooklyn on October 1st, 1st and 2nd respectively. The Dixie transported one company of four officers and 123 men from San Juan to Havana to complete the quota of the battalions. While this movement was in process, the Atlantic Fleet assembled its Marine guards (804 officers and men), aboard the Kentucky and Indiana on September 24th, and despatched them to Havana. This latter force, together with the five battalions mentioned before, gave a total strength of 97 officers and 2,795 men, which was organized into the First Provisional Brigade with Colonel L.W.T. Waller, U.S.M.C., commanding. This unit functioned under naval jurisdiction until November 1st. Prior to this date many of the Marine guards had been returned to their respective ships, or sent to stations in the United States. On November 1st the First Provisional Brigade was disbanded, the First Provisional Regiment formed therefrom, was detached for duty with the Army of Cuban Pacification under Army jurisdiction, and remained on such duty until January 23, 1909 when it returned to the United States.

President Theodore (Teddy) Roosevelt, in his message to Congress on December 3, 1906, wrote: "It was owing in large part to the General Board that the Navy was able at the outset to meet the Cuban crisis with such instant efficiency; ship after ship appearing on the shortest notice at any threatened point, while the Marine Corps in particular performed indispensable service."

(1912)

Just about three years after the withdrawal of the Army of Cuban Pacification this island showed distinct signs

(Cuba)

of again breaking forth in revolution. With an idea of fore-stalling such an event if it had actually started, a force of Marines was ordered assembled and despatched to Cuban waters. Accordingly, a Provisional Brigade was formed under the command of Colonel Lincoln Karmany, consisting of the First Regiment, (Colonel Barnett), and Second Regiment, (Colonel Mahoney). The 1st Regiment sailed on the Prairie on May 23rd, while the 2nd Regiment was distributed on nine vessels of the Atlantic Fleet, (Georgia, Minnesota, Mississippi, Missouri, Nebraska, New Jersey, Ohio, Rhode Island, and Washington), and sailed on the 26th, and 27th for Key West. The Rhode Island and Washington sailed from Key West and arrived at Havana on the 10th of June. The Georgia and New Jersey remained at Key West during the month of June, while the Minnesota, Mississippi, Nebraska, and Ohio sailed from that place to Guantanamo Bay, Cuba, and landed on the 8th of June. Some of this force served in the interior.

The 1st Regiment landed at Guantanamo Bay on the 28th of May, and a few days later was distributed at different points in the eastern end of the island. With the exception of a battalion of two companies (that remained at Guantanamo Bay), the entire Brigade was returned to the United States on July 9th, 24th, and August 5th.

(1917)

Conditions remained rather tranquil for nearly five years before another outbreak occurred. In February of this year the political conditions were so turbulent that landing of American troops was again found necessary. On March 1st the following ships of the Atlantic Fleet landed their Marine detachments at various places, mostly in Oriente Province: Connecticut, 1-19; Machias, 1-31 and April 1-11; Michigan, 1-3; Montana, 1-22; New York, 3-7; Olympia, 8-16 and 18-22; South Carolina, 3-4 and 7-16; Texas, 7-10. In addition to these detachments, the 24th Company stationed at the Naval Station, Guantanamo Bay, was in the interior from March 1st to 27th. In August of this same year, the 7th Regiment of Marines, under command of Colonel M.J. Shaw, was ordered to the Naval Station, Guantanamo Bay, and went into camp at Deer Point. On October 24th, this Regiment commenced to move into the interior of Cuba, where its different units were stationed at San Juan Hill, Bayamo, Camaguey, Guantanamo City, and San Luis, all in Oriente Province. The movement of this unit into the interior was not primarily for the suppression

(Cuba)

of any revolutionary condition then existing, but was intended to have a beneficial effect toward minimizing the activities of agents of the Central powers who were known to be active in propaganda and sabotage operations. This regiment was withdrawn in August, 1919, with the exception of two companies which remained at Camaguey until February 15, 1922.

(1933)

In this year another upheaval took place in the political condition of this Island Republic. President Gerardo Machado was deposed and had to leave the country. However, the American Government decided to maintain a "hands-off" policy, and let the Cubans work out their own salvation. Ships of the United States Navy, with Marines aboard, were in close proximity to observe conditions, but did not make a landing.

References: Sec. Navy An. Rep; Major-General Commandant An. Rep; Marine Corps Muster Rolls; Marine Corps Archives.

DOMINICAN REPUBLIC

(1800)

Every United States Marine should have indelibly impressed upon his mind a picture of the island which now contains the Dominican Republic, because the city of Puerto Plata (Port au Platte), in this republic is the birth-place of the history of the Landings, other than in time of war, of his Corps. Less than two years had elapsed since the reorganization of the Marine Corps before its personnel began to make this history, which was to be recorded in the pages of America's notable achievements. And Captain Daniel Carmick with his Marines of the frigate Constitution was the means employed to this end.

Commodore Silas Talbot, one of the first captains of the United States Navy, was cruising on the Santo Domingo Station in the early part of this year. During this cruise he conceived and carried out one of the most daring deeds ever recorded in the annals of the United States Navy – that of cutting out a valuable French letter of marque, which was then lying in the harbor of Puerto Plata under the protection of the guns of the forts. Until recently this vessel had been the British packet Sandwich, and she was thought to have a most valuable cargo aboard.

The frigate Constitution drew too much water for the enterprize and it was therefore necessary that a ship of less draft be found in order to carry out the Commodore's plan. An American sloop, the Sally, was located in the vicinity, and was impressed into service for the expedition. Captain Carmick and his Marines, together with a detachment of sailors from the Constitution, were embarked aboard the Sally, with Lieutenant Isaac Hull in command, and the force got underway.

The Sally, under Lieutenant Hull, sailed in broad daylight, into the harbor on May 12th, and found the Sandwich lying with her broadside bearing on the approach under the guns of a battery on shore to protect her. The determined party of Americans in the sloop, not in the least deterred by this formal array of armament, ran the Sandwich aboard, and carried her without the loss of a man. As soon as her capture was assured, Captain Carmick and his Marines, pulled to the shore, made a landing near the battery, captured it, spiked the guns, and then returned aboard the captured vessel before the enemy could summon reinforcements from the town. The attack had been so sudden and determined,

(Dominican Republic)

and the shore authorities were so awed by the audacity of the Americans, that they made but a feeble attempt to regain the vessel.

The landing party immediately set about preparing the captured vessel for sea but, owing to the absence of a sufficient breeze to make headway from the harbor, they were compelled to wait until the following morning, the 13th, before they could sail their ship, and the captured vessel out to sea, and safety. Thus was the first deed in the history of the Landings of United States Marines recorded.

(1903)

Political unrest and revolutionary disturbances, with frequent overturns of government, begun as early as 1808, had been continued through the succeeding years, and in this year the country was again in a political and social upheaval, which threatened the lives and property of all foreigners then within its boundaries.

The American Consul-General, Campbell L. Maxwell, being apprehensive for the safety of citizens of the United States, applied to Commander William H. Turner, of the Atlanta, then in Dominican waters, for a guard of Marines to be landed; to which the Commander readily agreed. First Lieutenant Richard G. McConnell was in command of the Marine detachment aboard the Atlanta, and he, together with 25 of his men, were detailed to proceed ashore to the American Consulate to insure its protection as well as the lives of foreigners. This force was landed on April 1st, and remained so employed until the 19th when it was withdrawn.

(1904)

The cause for the landing of United States forces in January and February had its inception in the latter part of the previous year. In September of that year, the Dominican Government announced its intention of establishing the neutrality of Dominican waters, and of making certain ports free, to the exclusion of others. To this Mr. Powell, the American Minister, made a strong protest, and the bill was withdrawn. In October, the American mail steamer Cherokee was stopped off Puerto Plata, and a permit to enter the harbor refused, but she ran the so-called blockade and discharged her cargo. In November a Clyde line steamer was fired upon by the Dominican cruiser Presidente, off Samana.

(Dominican Republic)

The insurrectionists apparently redoubled their efforts and on the 24th of November, the capital surrendered, and President Wos y Gil and his cabinet fled to a German warship for refuge. A provisional government was then established under the leadership of Carlos F. Morales, but this was no sooner established than a new revolution began, headed by a former president, Jiminez. Morales was not yet deposed, however. The revolutionists perpetrated numerous indignities upon Americans, destroying their property, killing of live stock, destroying sugar cane on American owned plantations, and intercepting vessels of the Clyde Line Steamship Company - notably, the case of the steamer New York at Monte Cristi. Conditions in and around Sosua and Puerto Plata were in such a serious state that Commander Albert C. Dillingham, in the Detroit, proceeded from Port of Spain, Trinidad, to the latter place to protect American citizens and their property. He arrived on January 1st and on the 3rd despatched a Marine detachment ashore to enforce a prohibition of fighting within a defined area containing United States citizens. Leaving this detachment on shore, he then proceeded to Sosua where he landed a detachment of ten men on the 7th, under Ensign Caffery to protect the American Consulate. In the afternoon of the same day he returned to Puerto Plata, withdrew the Marines which had been landed there on the 3rd, and again returned to Sosua.

The British Government had noted the apparent seriousness of the revolutionary movement in Santo Domingo and had despatched H.B.M.S. Pallas, under the command of Commander C. Hope Robertson as their representative at this place. Commanders Dillingham and Robertson collaborated in establishing protective zones against the operations of the opposing Dominican factions. On the 15th the Marine detachment which had been landed at Sosua on the 7th was withdrawn, and the Detroit proceeded to Puerto Plata. On the morning of the 17th the opposing forces engaged in a pitched battle causing the Jiminez soldiers to retreat to the fort, firing as they ran. In the meantime the Hartford had arrived to reinforce the Detroit, and upon this serious outbreak of firing, Commander Dillingham deemed it advisable to despatch a considerable force on shore for the protection of the lives of all foreign residents. Accordingly, the Marine Guard and a detachment of sailors were despatched early in the morning, while the Hartford "sent half of landing party ashore." About mid-afternoon this landing party returned to their respective ships, with the exception of the Marine Guard of the Detroit, which remained ashore to guard the American Consulate until the 23rd.

On the 1st of February an incident took place which decided the United States Government to despatch an armed

(Dominican Republic) 68

force to the Dominican Republic in order that adequate protection might be afforded its citizens. This affair was the firing upon and killing of a member of the crew (J.C. Johnston) of the launch from the auxiliary cruiser Yankee, then at Santo Domingo City, by the Revolutionary forces under Jiminez.

Captain Richard Wainwright, who was temporarily in command of the South Atlantic Squadron, was ordered to proceed to the troubled area, on the 8th of February, and he arrived at Santo Domingo City, aboard the Newark, on the 11th, finding that the Columbia had preceded him, having arrived on the 8th. Prior to the arrival of Captain Wainwright, Captain James M. Miller, of the Columbia, who was senior to Captain Wainwright, had sent an officer and a Marine sergeant ashore to confer with the insurgents relative to the entry of the Clyde Line steamer New York, into the harbor to discharge her cargo. This was on the 9th, and on the 11th, after the arrival of Captain Wainwright, the steamer New York stood in under convoy of the steam launch of the Columbia, and when near the dock the insurgents fired upon and struck the steamer several times; some of the bullets grazing the launch, which was flying the American flag.

This was a flagrant violation of an armistice which was supposed to be in force between the contending parties, and Captain Miller was apparently determined not to let such an incident pass without exacting redress for the insult to the American flag. A conference was held aboard the Columbia, and it was decided to shell the insurgents' position and then land Marines and bluejackets from both ships. Having informed the government authorities, and the American Charge' de Affaires of this intention, the Newark opened fire at 3:25 p.m., and ten minutes later the landing forces left for the shore. Each ship despatched one battalion of approximately 160 officers and men, including the Marines under the command of Captain Albert S. McLemore (Newark) and First Lieutenant Henry D.F. Long (Columbia), the whole force being under the direct command of the Executive Officer of the Columbia, Lieutenant-Commander James P. Parker.

The boats carrying this landing force had nearly reached the beach, when they were fired upon by the insurgent forces from shore, but no casualties were suffered. They pushed on, however, and landed at 4:30 p.m. When the

(Dominican Republic)

insurgents' fire was observed from the deck of the Columbia, orders were issued to open a bombardment on their position from the 4-inch guns, and the first shot was fired at 4:32 and was continued until 4:47. The fire from the Newark was continued until 5:00 p.m., when the bombardment ceased. The landing force returned to their respective ships between 9:00 and 10:00 that night.

(1916)

The de facto governments which had ruled the affairs of the republic since the last declaration of its independence in February 1844, and more particularly that under the leadership of Ulises Heureaux (1882-89), had borrowed from foreign governments until the finances were in such a state as to make the repayment of loans an impossibility unless the revenues received were controlled by some responsible party or foreign state. Under this state of affairs, and at the request of the Dominican government, the United States took over control of the Dominican finances in 1905.

Between the years of 1911 and the present, no fewer than six presidents held office for various periods of time. In the early part of this year, the Dominican government was in a state of collapse. General Arias, who was then Secretary of War, launched an insurrection against the government headed by Juan Isidro Jiminez, and a state of anarchy followed.

The contending forces were actively engaged in contending for the possession of the capital, Santo Domingo City, and the American Legation being in the direct line of fire, was struck several times by shells fired from the guns of these forces. Advices as to this state of affairs were furnished the State Department by the American Minister, William W. Russell, and the Navy Department, in turn, was requested to despatch a naval force to the troubled area to furnish protection for United States citizens.

Rear Admiral William B. Caperton, commanding the Cruiser Force, ordered the 6th and 9th companies of Marines from Haiti to the naval transport Prairie, despatched it to Santo Domingo City, and upon its arrival May 5th, these companies were landed. A little later this force was reinforced by the 1st, 4th, 5th, 13th, 14th, 19th, and 24th Marine companies, and Santo Domingo City was occupied. This caused the withdrawal of the forces under General Arias, who re-established his headquarters at Santiago in the interior.

Admiral Caperton requested the Navy Department to send an additional regiment of Marines, for service in conjunction with those already landed, in order to quickly put down the revolution and effect the pacification of the interior. The 4th Regiment of Marines, under Colonel Joseph H. Pendleton, ordered from San Diego, arrived at Monte Cristi and disembarked on June 21st. Marines from the <u>New Jersey</u> and <u>Rhode Island</u> had been landed previously at Puerto Plata, as well as some of the companies originally landed at Santo Dominto City, including the artillery battalion which landed at Monte Cristi.

When Colonel Pendleton arrived with the 4th Regiment, he was designated to command all forces ashore, and combining his force with the other Marine Companies and detachments then on shore, he was directed to start an expedition to the interior, capture Santiago (Arias' Headquarters), and in this manner bring about tranquil conditions. The Expedition started on its mission on the 26th, headed by Colonel Pendleton, himself. Before he reached his objective however, a peace commission had negotiated an agreement whereby the revolutionists would lay down their arms, and a provisional government would be organized. The expedition then advanced into Santiago without further opposition, entering the city on July 6th.

Every effort was made on the part of the American government to negotiate a treaty which would safeguard the tranquility of the Republic, and the performance of its established treaty obligations. These efforts met with failure. Consequently, the United States proclaimed a military occupation and military government in Santo Domingo from November 29th. This government was organized upon the usual plan - Foreign Relations, Finance, Public Works and Communications, Justice and Public Instruction, Agriculture and Immigration, and Interior (under which was the Department of War and Navy). The Department of Sanitation was subsequently established. The military government brought order out of chaos, and placed the government on a sound basis in all respects.

On October 21, 1922, a provisional government was installed, and all of the functions of civil government were delivered into its hands. The Military Governor was charged with the approval of expenditures not provided for in the budget, and the task of quelling disturbances when, in his opinion and in the opinion of the Provisional Government, the local constabulary was unable to cope with it.

Regular elections having been previously held, a constitutional government was inaugurated at 10:30 a.m. July 12, 1924; Fort Ozama was turned over to the new Govern-

(Dominican Republic)

ment in the afternoon, and the American forces commenced their withdrawal. This withdrawal was completed on September 17, 1924.

The Military Governorship was held, respectively, by Rear Admiral Harry S. Knapp, Rear Admiral Thomas Snowden, Rear Admiral Samuel S. Robison, and Brigadier General Harry Lee of the United States Marines, whose tenure of office was from December 5, 1922, to the withdrawal of all troops.

During the occupation the Marines were divided into detachments and placed at strategic places in order to put an end to banditry, which had grown to serious proportions due to the absence of civil government. This situation was soon under control. The American forces varied in strength from the 280 who first landed, to three regiments (3rd, 4th, and 15th) of approximately 3,000 officers and men. The Marines suffered casualties of 4 officers and 10 men killed, 1 officer and 1 man died of wounds, 3 officers and 51 men died of disease, 2 officers and 37 men died through accident, 2 officers and 29 men died due to other causes, and 5 officers and 50 men were wounded in action.

In October, 1917, a Guardia (or Constabulary) was organized, officered and trained by the Marines, and used extensively in subduing bandit activities throughout the island. Upon the withdrawal of the United States forces, this organization took over all police duties of the Republic under their own officers.

References: Cooper's Hist. Navy, I, 364; Collum's Hist. U.S. Marine Corps, 45; St. Dept. Archives; Marine Corps Archives; Navy Archives; Sec. Navy An. Rep., 1903, 1229; id., 1904, 540; id., 1916, 764-765; The Dom. Rep., Conf. Reg. No. 167, Navy Dept; Logs of Atlanta, Detroit, Newark, and Columbia.

DRUMMONDS ISLAND
(1841)

    In the early spring of this year Lieutenant William L. Hudson, commanding the Peacock of the Wilkes Exploring Expedition, was surveying in the vicinity of this island. A member of his crew had related the narrative of a vessel which had been wrecked on this Island some time previously, her captain and crew massacred, the vessel plundered of everything of value, but that the wife and child of the captain were saved, and were supposed to be living on the island. This individual also stated that he had been a member of the crew of another ship which had endeavored, without success, to rescue the woman and child, and that the facts were contained in a journal kept on board this vessel. (Note. An entry in the log of the Peacock is as follows: "(the journal is on board).").

    Apparently Lieutenant Hudson was quite satisfied as to the authenticity of this account, for he brought his ship to anchor, on April 6th, about four and one-half miles from the town of Utirod (where the catastrophe was supposed to have occurred), armed four boats, under Lieutenant Perry, and together with "the Scientific Corps, two or three other officers" and himself made a landing the object of which was "to make some observations on the Dip and Intensity as well as determine the Lat & Long - also to give the Scientific Gents an opportunity of gathering such information as might be picked up - and to ascertain if there lives or had lived on the Island a White Woman said to have been taken from a vessel some time since - which vessel was wrecked on the reef off the NW pt and all on board massacred excepting the Capts wife & child."

    Upon reaching the beach, Lieutenant Hudson and party were met by a great number of natives, "old and young - males & Females who cordially took us by the hand and lead (led) us to the Town house - situated near the water." Inquiries were made "about the woman" but no information could be obtained. They did learn, however, that a vessel had been wrecked, and in some of the huts "parts of the vessel was found." Many of the houses were closed to the Americans, and no amount of persuasion on their part could induce the natives to open them. There seemed to be "a visible mystery in the whole affair."

    After several hours rambling about the town, and with the approach of evening, the American party returned to the Peacock, informing the natives they would reappear the following day. Apparently Lieutenant Hudson was not ready to acknowledge defeat in the finding of the white woman. About 3:00 p.m. the 7th, he in his gig, accompanied by four armed boats, paid another visit to the village. He and his

(Drummonds Island)

party remained ashore for about four hours, when he decided to return to his ship. Upon reaching his boats he found that one of his party, "Jno Anderson", was missing, and it was feared that he had been decoyed away and massacred by the natives. Before the party left the shore, a diligent search was made and a reward offered, but the natives took no notice. Instead, they exhibited every sign of hostility. Many having armed themselves, they began to collect around the Americans with the evident intention of "taking the boats." As the boats shoved off from shore, the natives began to stone them, at the same time brandishing their spears and swords in the air.

Lieutenant Hudson waited for two days, but Anderson did not return, and the fears previously entertained now seemed a certainty - Anderson must have been foully murdered. The Lieutenant decided to attack the town and administer condign punishment for the outrage upon the member of his crew. Having a Marine Guard at his disposal, he selected the Marines, and members of his crew, to the number of about 80 men, armed and equipped them, divided them into three units under the "command of Walker," (undoubtedly Lieut. Wm. M. Walker), and at daylight the 9th (April), were ready to land. The schooner Flying Fish, which had arrived the day before, was ordered inshore to cover the party in the boats, seven in number, as a haven for the landing party should they be driven back by the natives. The landing party had not proceeded far before they perceived about "6 or 800" natives collected on or near the beach, brandishing their weapons, at the same time going through a war dance, and beckoning the comparatively small party of Americans onward with the evident intention of concluding forthwith the coming battle between the unequal forces. The determined Americans pushed on notwithstanding, and when within a few yards of the shore laid on their oars and demanded the surrender of Anderson. The natives paid little or no heed to the demand, but instead began to wade out into the water with the apparent intention of surrounding the boats of the landing party. Seeing this, Lieutenant Walker ordered a retreat for a short distance and then fired a "Rocket" into the midst of the milling crowd of natives on shore. This unlooked-for method of combat so terrified them that they immediately "fled to the Bush." However, their terror was of short duration, for they soon began to return from all quarters with heightened fury, and fanatic cries of rage. The boats now advanced to within "pistol shot" and fired a volley of musketry into the mob. Several were seen to fall, apparently wounded, when all others save one, who appeared to be the chief and who was covered "with armour," fled in much disorder, followed by additional volleys from the muskets of the Marines and sailors. The party now landed, and im-

(Drummonds Island)

mediately set about the destruction of the village. The "Town house" received first consideration, and it was soon enveloped in flames. Other parts of the town were then set afire and, caught by a stiff breeze, the flames spread rapidly until every hut was being consumed by the conflagration, and in less than two hours the whole village of some 300 houses had been reduced to ashes.

The destruction of the first village having been accomplished the landing party turned to the next - Aita. This received the same fate as the first, and, it, too, was soon consumed by flames. Neither Anderson, nor the "White Woman" and child, had been found, so the Americans lingered in an endeavor to obtain some information as to their ultimate fate. In this, however, they were destined to disappointment, and were compelled to retrace their steps with the mystery still unsolved. Believing that nothing more could be accomplished by remaining longer on the island, Lieutenant Walker ordered a return to the boats, regaining which they repaired aboard the Peacock, and the two American vessels took their departure from the ill-fated Island.

Reference: Log of Peacock.

E G Y P T

(1882)

Admiral Seymour, of the British Navy, bombarded the forts and city of Alexandria on July 11th of this year. Prior to this time, Rear Admiral Nicholson, of the American Navy, had received orders to proceed to that place to observe conditions and, if necessary, take such action as might be needed for the protection of American interests. He arrived in his flagship, the Lancaster, on the 27th of June, and was later joined by the Quinnebaug and Nipsic on July 1st and 12th, respectively.

As a consequence of the bombardment by the British the city was in a state of anarchy; murder, fire, pillage and rapine reigned, foreigners being the particular object for the visitation of these outrages. Admiral Nicholson decided that for humanity's sake, some action on his part was necessary. He consulted with the British Admiral on the 14th and, upon his return to the Lancaster, issued orders for a landing party. Accordingly 73 Marines, officers and men, from the three American ships, under Captain Henry C. Cochrane and Lieutenants L.W.T. Waller and Frank L. Denny, augmented by 57 sailors, officers and men, were despatched ashore to assist in restoring order, prevent further destruction, fight the fire that was raging, re-establish the American consulate, and look after American interests in general.

The Marines were the first foreign troops to enter Alexandria after the bombardment. The British soon followed with a force of about 4,000, under command of Captain Fisher. Other foreign troops followed soon after the American and British landings.

Admiral Nicholson opened his ships as a shelter for refugees during the bombardment and for some time thereafter. This offer was promptly accepted, and men, women and children of all walks of life, were administered to be the American men-o-wars-men. This kind and friendly act was not soon forgotten.

Conditions so improved ashore that the sailors were returned to their respective ships on the 15th, and by the 20th all of the Marines had returned, except a detail from the Quinnebaug, under Lieutenant Denny, which remained until the 24th. The Lancaster and Nipsic departed on the 20th of July, and the Quinnebaug on the 29th of August.

References: Collum's Hist. U.S. Marine Corps, 232-234; Marine Corps Archives; Navy Archives; Logs of Lancaster, Quinnebaug and Nipsic.

FALKLAND ISLANDS

(1831)

For several years sealing around these islands had been a profitable trade. American sealers, like those of other countries, had been engaged in this enterprize for some time. During the latter part of this year the American schooners <u>Breakwater</u>, <u>Harriet</u>, and <u>Superior</u>, were so employed when seized by Luis Vernet, the political and military governor of the islands. This act was referred to by President Andrew Jackson in his annual message to Congress of December 6, 1831, as "a band acting, as they pretend, under the authority of the Government of Buenos Ayres," and recommended the adoption of measures "for providing a force adequate to the complete protection of our fellow-citizens fishing and trading in those seas."

It was quite evident that Congress approved of the President's recommendation, inasmuch as the sloop <u>Lexington</u>, under Commander Silas Duncan, was ordered from Buenos Ayres to the Falklands to release these American schooners. Commander Duncan arrived off Berkley Sound on the morning of December 28th, and at 12:15 p.m. came to anchor in the Sound, (having taken in tow a small schooner a short way from the entrance), where he remained apparently inactive until January 1, 1832.

(1832)

Early in the morning of the first day of the year, he stood in for the port of St. Louis and came to anchor at 11:30 a.m. Just prior to anchoring, he sent a landing party of two officers and fifteen men, (presumably Marines), ashore in the commandeered schooner to confer with the authorities, and, at 11:45, another party, well armed, in two boats, to augment the first. The three schooners were finally liberated, and permitted to proceed.

Practically all of the American citizens in the islands desired to leave, and Commander Duncan agreed to give them passage to Montevideo in the <u>Lexington</u>. While they were preparing for their departure, he sent a guard of 12 Marines ashore to protect their property, and to assist them in their preparations for the voyage. This guard returned at noon the following day, but a smaller guard went ashore each day until the 5th. On the 21st those Americans who wished to leave the Island came aboard the <u>Lexington</u>, and were made as confortable as conditions on board a man of war would permit. The following day this party, consisting of 20 men, 8 women and 10 children sailed on board the <u>Lexington</u> for their native land.

References: Moore's Int. Law Dig., I, 298-299; Log of
   <u>Lexington</u>; Marine Corps Archives; Sec. Navy An. Rep.,
   1831, 5,253.

FEEJEE ISLANDS
(1840)

For some time prior to this year, the United States government had been considering an expedition to the South Seas, in the interests of science, commerce and navigation. Especially anxious were they to determine the existence, and accurate location, of doubtful islands and shoals which were thought to be in the track of American trading vessels plying the Pacific.

In furtherance of this plan Congress authorized a small squadron of vessels of the navy to be used for this purpose. The Navy Department selected Lieutenant Charles Wilkes to head the expedition, and designated the sloops of war Vincennes and Peacock, the brig Porpoise, the storeship Relief and the tenders Flying-Fish and Sea-Gull, to comprise the squadron, and issued instructions for the expedition on August 11, 1838. Preliminary preparations having been made the corps of scientific men repaired aboard, and everything else being in readiness, the squadron sailed from Hampton Roads on August 19th. About mid-summer of the following year (1839), the expedition arrived in the Southern Archipelago, and one of the first steps taken by Commander Wilkes was to persuade the principal chiefs of the islands to enter into a form of treaty by the promulgation of certain Regulations for the conduct of both parties in future commercial relations. These negotiations were successful, and a set of "Commercial Regulations" were drawn up and signed by Commander Wilkes and the principal Chiefs of the Islands of Samoa and Feejee; those for the latter were signed on June 10, 1840.

These Regulations, however, were either not understood by the natives, or else they chose to disregard them, for on July 12th an incident took place in violation of the Regulations, which necessitated the use of force to obtain redress. On the morning of the 12th a surveying party in the Launch and First Cutter of the Vincennes under Lieutenant Perry were compelled to put into Sualib Bay for shelter during a sudden squall. As soon as the storm was over, the party started to beat out to sea again but, in doing so, the rudder of the Cutter was damaged and she drifted on the reef. The Launch, being farther out, was not endangered. No sooner was the damaged boat grounded than she was surrounded by a large number of natives, who manifested hostile dispositions against the Americans. Recourse to arms was out of the question, due to the fact that everything in the boat was drenched during the storm. They were obliged to abandon her, taking only the surveying instruments, and repairing to the Launch for their own safety. The natives now dragged the Cutter up on the beach, and stripped her of everything of value. But for the fact that

(Feejee Islands)

the Launch had two native chiefs aboard as pilots, the crew of the Cutter might have fared much worse at the hands of the hostile mob.

The Launch, with the rescued crew of the Cutter aboard, returned to the Vincennes about noon, and reported the facts of the affair to Lieutenant Wilkes, who decided to avenge this outrage immediately. He took the Flying-Fish with ten pulling boats, loaded them with the Marines from the two ships (Vincennes and Peacock), and a detachment of sailors, and proceeded to the scene of the mishap of the cutter. They entered the Bay, landed the force, and marched to the village, the inhabitants although unusually well supplied with firearms, offering no resistance. The town, consisting of about sixty huts of flimsy construction, was fired and burnt to the ground, as a lesson to the savages. This accomplished, the force returned to their ships. Later in the same month, however, it was again necessary for Lieutenant Wilkes to avenge a more serious outrage against the Americans - that of the murder of Lieutenant Joseph A. Underwood, and Midshipman Wilkes Henry, nephew of Lieutenant Wilkes.

On the 23rd of July the surveying party under Lieutenant James Alden, with Lieutenant Underwood and Midshipman Henry, was at work near the island of Malolo and, as Lieutenant Underwood desired to signal the Porpoise, he went ashore to a high peak to look for her. He was soon recalled, in consequence of some suspicious movements among the natives, bringing a native boy as hostage. The following morning, the 24th, he again landed for the purpose of procuring provisions. The natives were reluctant about trading, so he remained on shore some length of time in unsuccessful attempts at negotiation. In the mean time Midshipman Henry had joined the rest of the American party on shore. The natives began to collect in large numbers, and manifested intentions of attacking the Americans. Seeing this, Underwood ordered a retreat to the boat. At the same time the native hostage jumped from the boat, made for the shore, and escaped. Simultaneously the report of firearms was heard ashore, by the party which had remained in the boat. They believed this indicated that Lieutenant Underwood was in trouble, so they pushed for the land, and as soon as their firearms bore effectively, the savages disappeared in hasty retreat. When they had reached the beach they found one seaman badly wounded, and Lieutenant Underwood and Midshipman Henry lying prostrate on the ground, the latter two expiring a few moments later. The bodies of the two officers and the wounded seaman were carried to the boat, and the whole party returned to the Flying-Fish a few miles distant.

(Feejee Islands)

Lieutenant Wilkes was aboard the last named vessel, and had the _Porpoise_ in company. When he was advised of this unprovoked massacre he determined to make it his business to see that stern retribution be visited upon the natives of the island. Accordingly, he selected a force of Marines and sailors to patrol in boats around the island to prevent the escape of any of the natives until he had attended to the sad duty of laying to rest the remains of the unfortunate officer, Lieutenant Underwood and Midshipman Henry, which was done on the 25th. The natives made several attempts to escape, but the Americans drove them back each time "at the point of the bayonet."

There were two villages on the island - Sualib, on the southern end, and Arro on the opposite end. Lieutenant Wilkes planned to send a landing party of Marines and sailors, under Lieutenant Cadwalader Ringgold, to attack Sualib while he, himself, would remain with the boats, prevent the natives from escaping, proceed to Arro, and cooperate with the shore party in the attack and capture of this village. On the 26th this plan was carried into execution. The party under Lieutenant Ringgold, numbering about 70 officers, Marines and sailors, landed on the southeast point of the island, destroyed the plantations in their course, and crossing over the high land finally came in sight of Sualib, their first objective. Here the natives had assembled with the evident intention to defend themselves by all means possible. Their preparation and position was not to be despised, even by disciplined troops. The town was surrounded by a strong stockade of cocoanut trees, on the outside of which was a wide ditch filled with water, and on the inside a dry ditch, in which the natives were entrenched.

As soon as the Americans came within effective rifle fire of the stockade, they opened a sharp attack for about fifteen minutes, during which a chief and six of the savages were killed, and the houses within fired by a rocket. The natives, apparently terrified by the conflagration among their huts, began to escape through a gate, leading toward the sea, in utmost consternation and confusion. A few of the American party were wounded, but only one severely. Lieutenant Ringgold and his party finished the destruction of the village, and then proceeded across the island to Arro. Upon reaching this place, however, he found that Lieutenant Wilkes, with his own party in the boats, had preceded him and, meeting no resistance, had completely destroyed the village. The next day the whole force from

(Feejee Islands)

the vessels assembled on a hill, and received a large delegation who came to sue for pardon for the crime they had committed in murdering the American officers. Lieutenant Wilkes now believed that the natives would henceforth respect all people of the White race, who might by accident or otherwise happen to be in their domain. The punishment administered was severe, but, in his opinion, merited by the circumstances.

(1855)

For about fifteen years after the occurrences above related, the Feejee Islanders kept fresh in the memory the lesson taught them by Lieutenant Wilkes. However, being natives of a tropical climate, and subject to the inertia usually attributed to such inhabitants, the effects of the lesson so administered finally waned and disappeared.

In the summer of this year the American sloop of war John Adams, under command of Commander Edward B. Boutwell, was cruising about the south Pacific islands on her regular mission, that of protecting American interests. While she was at Samoa, Commander Boutwell received instructions to proceed to the Feejee group, to seek reparations for various wrongs inflicted upon Americans residing at the islands, and upon shipwrecked seamen. These instructions he immediately proceeded to execute. On the 12th of September he arrived at the Island of Nukulau, made a landing with Marines (under Lieutenant John L. Broome) and sailors, (in two boats, including a boat howitzer), made a circuit of the island, and then returned to the ship. He next visited Rewa, Island of Viti Levu, where he remained until the 26th. While here (on the 22nd), Commander Boutwell sent an armed party to Bau, in two boats, for the purpose of securing the person of Tui Viti, King of Feejee, to persuade him to sign a treaty promising to pay certain sums of money due American citizens for loss and destruction of their property. Late in the afternoon the boats returned, bringing the king with them, and accompanied by about 300 natives in canoes, which were moored to the stern of the vessel. Apparently the king was kept aboard the sloop until the 25th, for on that date, having signed the treaty in the meantime, he was permitted to return to his village.

The American Consul, Mr. John B. Williams, paid a visit to Commander Boutwell on the 16th, remained aboard over night, and left for shore the next morning, receiving a salute of 9 guns upon leaving the John Adams. On the 20th, the Commander, who was apparently in need of fresh meat, "sent party on the Island to cut wood, and to shoot a bullock."

(Feejee Islands)

On the morning of the 25th (September), the sloop sailed for Levuka Harbor, Island of Ovalau, arriving there early the next morning. She remained here until October 27th, when she returned to the Bay of Luva, Viti Levu, at which place she arrived at 5:00 p.m. the same date. It seems that Chief Tui Viti (king) had not kept his promise, and it was therefore necessary for Commander Boutwell to resort to additional means to revivify what he had so sadly neglected. The following afternoon (28th), the 2nd and 3rd cutters were fully armed, under the command of Lieutenant Benjamin F. Shattuck, left the ship, and proceeded toward the town of Namula. About an hour later the cutters were followed by the Launch, under Acting Master Badger, who was accompanied by several other officers "and Consul Williams", and proceeded to the town of Vutia.

The launch returned to the ship at 4:30 p.m. the following day, the 29th, having "burnt" the town of Vutia, but the time that the cutters returned is not stated. However, it was prior to 9:00 a.m. of the 30th, for at that hour they left the ship on another mission to the town of Lassalassa. Soon after this reinforcements were sent to their assistance from the ship, as that force was heavily engaged with the natives. This landing force of Marines and sailors was under the direct command of Lieutenant Louis C. Sartori, and remained on shore until shortly after 4:00 p.m. the 31st. The party had roundly chastized the natives, and burned two of their villages, but not, however, without loss to themselves, for Landsman Charles Lockwood had been killed, and Corporal John Johnson, of the Marines, and Charles Beck were wounded.

Believing that the natives had been taught a lesson to be remembered, and conditions having settled to normal, the Commander took his departure on November 4th.

(1858)

Conditions in this group of islands remained tranquil for the next three years, when it became necessary to administer another chastizement to the natives, for outrages perpetrated against American citizens. Sometime during the middle of the year, two American citizens had been murdered on the Island of Waya (Waia), while following the pursuits of legitimate trade. This information came to the attention of Commander Arthur Sinclair, of the sloop Vandalia, which was then at Lavuka (Lavouka), Island of Ovalou. The American schooner Mechanic (under charter by the United States), being also in the harbor, the Commander, having planned an expedition to Waya, decided to use her instead of his own vessel, owing to the difference in the draught of the two ships.

(Feejee Islands)

The Mechanic was prepared in all respects for the trip, a landing force of 10 Marines under Lieutenant Alan Ramsay, together with 4 Naval officers and 40 sailors, all under the command of Lieutenant C.H.B. Caldwell, sailed for Waya on the 6th of October. Lieutenant Caldwell, upon arrival at his destination, made a demand for the perpetrators of the murders but the chief defiantly refused, and assumed a very hostile attitude toward the American party. When the Lieutenant found that diplomacy was of no avail he determined to force compliance by other methods.

While the diplomatic negotiations were in progress some 300 native warriors gathered in the neighborhood, and things looked serious for the small party of Americans. However, this show of hostility by a much superior force of savages did not daunt the spirit of the little party from the Mechanic, who were determined to avenge the murder of their countrymen at all costs. A fierce conflict between the contending forces ensued, but was concluded eventually by the natives making a hasty retreat. Lieutenant Caldwell and his party remained on the Island for about ten days – returning to the Vandalia on the 16th. His mission had been accomplished without casualties to the Americans.

References: Logs of Vincennes, John Adams, Vandalia and Peacock; St. Dept. Archives; Memo Solic. St. Dept., 56; Collum's Hist. U.S. Marine Corps, 110-111; Hamersly, Gen. Reg., 100 Years, for names of officers; Marine Corps Archives; Marine Corps Muster Rolls; Navy Archives; Cooper's Hist. Navy, 45-47.

ONE HUNDRED EIGHTY LANDINGS OF UNITED STATES MARINES

1800 - 1934

A BRIEF HISTORY IN TWO PARTS

PART TWO

By

CAPTAIN HARRY ALANSON ELLSWORTH, U. S. MARINE CORPS

OFFICER IN CHARGE, HISTORICAL SECTION

FIRST EDITION
1934

(FORMOSA to URUGUAY)

FORMOSA ISLAND

(1867)

In the early months of this year the American bark Rover, while engaged in regular commerce among the island groups of the South Pacific, was wrecked on the southeast end of Formosa, and it was rumored that her crew had been murdered. This information reached Rear Admiral Henry H. Bell, commander-in-chief, Asiatic Squadron, and he ordered Commander John C. Febiger, in the Ashuelot, to proceed to the locality, gain such information as possible, and rescue the survivors should any be found. He arrived at Tai-wan-Foo in April; made known his mission, demanded an investigation of the outrage, the seizure and punishment of those implicated, and the recovery of any of the crew who survived. After considerable delay on the part of the authorities, and after many expressions of their willingness to comply, they finally advised Commander Febiger that they were unable to bring the perpetrators to justice, because they belonged to a horde of savages not obedient to their laws. The Commander deemed his force insufficient to resort to hostile measures with these savages, so he returned and reported to Admiral Bell, with such information as he had gained.

The Admiral was not disposed that so great a crime should pass unpunished, and therefore left Shanghai in June, with the Hartford, (his flagship) and the Wyoming, with the intention of destroying the lurking places of the savages responsible for the murder of the crew of the Rover. When he reached Taka, he received on board Mr. Pickering (an interpreter), Mr. Taylor (a merchant), and the British consul, Charles Carroll, who was anxious to accompany the expedition. Mr. Carroll had humanely but unsuccessfully endeavored to communicate with the savages, and ransom any of the crew of the Rover who survived.

On the 13th of June, the Admiral brought his ships to anchor within half a mile of the beach, and immediately sent a landing force ashore. This force consisted of Captain James Forney with 43 of his Marines, and 135 naval officers and men, commanded by Commander George C. Belknap, with Lieutenant-Commander Alexander S. Mackenzie as assistant. Soon after landing, savages dressed in clouts and their bodies painted, were by the aid of field glasses, seen assembled in parties on the cleared hills about two miles distant, their muskets glittering in the sun. As the landing party ascended the hills, the savages descended to meet them and, gliding through the high grass from cover to cover, displaying the strategy and courage of the American Indian. Delivering their fire, they retreated without being seen by the Americans, who, charging on their coverts, frequently

(Formosa Island)

fell into ambuscades. The landing party followed them until 2:00 p.m., when they halted to rest. The savages took this opportunity to approach and fire into the party. Lieutenant-Commander Mackenzie placed himself at the head of a company and charged into the ambuscade, receiving a mortal wound from which he died while being carried to the rear.

Several of the officers and men experienced severe sunstrokes, and as the command was generally exhausted, Commander Belknap decided to return to the ships, which were reached at 4:00 p.m., after a very trying march of six hours under a tropical sun. The experience obtained during this affair demonstrated the inutility of such an expedition against a savage enemy in a wild country, by sailors unaccustomed to ambuscades and bush life. Sailors, not being adapted to this kind of warfare, a different story might well have been written had the Admiral's force been composed entirely of Marines, who, because of the particular training they receive, are especially suited for missions of this nature.

Admiral Bell decided to make no further attempt by again landing his force. They had burned a number of native huts, chased them a considerable distance into the interior and inflicted severe punishment on the natives themselves. The expedition returned to Takao on the 14th, and there buried the remains of Mackenzie in the grounds of the British consulate.

References: Sec. Navy An. Rep., 1867, 7-9; Memo Solic. St. Dept., 58; Collum's Hist. U.S. Marine Corps, 196, 197; Logs of Hartford and Wyoming; Marine Corps Muster Rolls; Marine Corps Archives; Bu. Nav. Archives.

FRANCE

(1878)

The Universal Exposition of Paris which took place during this year was the scene of the first American Marine Guard to be stationed in France. A guard was deemed necessary for the protection of American exhibits, and the United States Marines were called upon to furnish the required number of men. First Lieutenant Benjamin R. Russell, and Second Lieutenant William F. Zeilin, with 29 enlisted Marines, were detailed for this duty. They embarked aboard the <u>Constitution</u> at Philadelphia, sailed on the 4th of March, and arrived at Havre, France, on the 3rd of the following month. A few days later they disembarked, proceeded to Paris where, upon arrival, they were quartered in the Caserne de Latour, Maubourg.

This special duty of guarding the American exhibits was continued until the 7th of January, 1879, when they returned to the <u>Constitution</u> for the return passage to the United States. The Honorable R.C. McCormick, commissioner for the United States, reported to the Navy Department that "their excellent conduct, both on and off duty, was spoken of in the most complimentary terms by the French authorities, by the citizens of Paris, and the visitors of the Exposition," and at the ceremonies attending the distribution of prizes, in October, their military bearing elicited "a grand outburst of enthusiasm, and they throughout reflected honor upon our flag by their admirable performance of an important duty in a foreign land."

(1889)

Another Exposition took place in Paris during this year and, because of the efficient manner in which the Marines had previously performed such duty, they were again called upon to furnish a guard for the American exhibits at this Exposition.

Captain Henry C. Cochrane, assisted by First Lieutenant Paul St. C. Murphy, and 30 enlisted Marines were detailed for this purpose. They embarked aboard the steamer <u>La Gascoigne</u>, arrived at Havre on the 21st of April, and at Paris the following day where they were quartered in the Ecole Militaire. The Exposition opened on the 6th of May with imposing ceremonies, and the detachment of American Marines received not only the applause of their countrymen, but the admiration of the French people and others present. On July 4th the Marines were marched to the grave of

(France)

Lafayette, and there, under the direction of Captain Cochrane, and in the presence of a large multitude, including the American Minister, Whitelaw Reid, General W.B. Franklin, Consul-General Rathbone and many others, the American Marines decorated with flowers the modest tomb of America's hero.

On the 19th of November the Marine detachment was honored by the presentation of medals by the American exhibitors; the officers' medals being of gold and those of the men of bronze. Captain Cochrane also had conferred upon him the decoration of Chevalier of the Legion of Honor, and complimented in a general order upon his return to the United States. This detachment, after having completed its special duty, returned to the Marine Barracks, Brooklyn, N.Y., where it arrived on the 23rd of December.

(1905)

Marines next had occasion to land on French soil when they arrived to escort the body of John Paul Jones, the naval hero of the American Revolution, back to his final resting place within the Naval Academy at Annapolis. The preliminary arrangements between the French and United States authorities having been concluded, Rear Admiral Charles D. Sigsbee (the same officer who commanded the ill-fated _Maine_ when she was blown up in the harbor of Havana, Cuba, in 1898,) was selected to head this unusual mission.

Admiral Sigsbee selected the _Brooklyn_ as his flagship, and together with the _Chattanooga_, _Galveston_, and _Tacoma_, each with its Marine detachment aboard, sailed from Tompkinsville, Staten Island, New York, on Sunday, June 18th. The squadron arrived at Cherbourg on the 30th, and on the following day Admiral Sigsbee, with his staff, proceeded by train to Paris, where he called upon the American ambassador, Robert S. McCormick, the French prime minister, M. Rouvier, the minister of marine, Mr. Thomson, and General Horace Porter, first special ambassador of the United States in connection with the transfer of the remains of John Paul Jones.

In the meantime Mr. Francis B. Loomis, second special ambassador of the United States, had arrived in Paris and, on July 4th, the American Ambassador, Admiral Sigsbee with his staff and Mr. Loomis were received by the President of France, M. Loubet. Upon leaving the palace, the American

(France)

officials were completely surrounded by a company of cuirassiers, forming the same escort which had been given the King of Spain on his first visit to the President of France during the preceding month.

The ceremonies incident to the actual transfer of the remains were scheduled to take place on the 6th of July. A few hours before daylight on this date, the Marines and sailors, constituting a force of about 500 officers and men, who were to participate, were landed from the ships at Cherbourg and boarded trains for Paris, where they arrived at about 11:40 the same forenoon. The Marines were under the command of Captain Theodore H. Low and Second Lieutenant Benjamin A. Lewis of the Brooklyn, First Lieutenant Theodore E. Backstrom of the Chattanooga, First Lieutenant Austin C. Rogers of the Galveston, and First Lieutenant Paul E. Chamberlain of the Tacoma. The enlisted Marines numbered 140.

At 3:30 in the afternoon the ceremonies took place at the American Church of the Holy Trinity where the remains were lying in state. The American Marines and sailors, and the French soldiers were formed outside of the church, where an artillery caisson was also in waiting. A memorial service was conducted by Reverend John B. Morgan, and at its conclusion, General Porter made a short address, transferring the remains to the second special ambassador, Mr. Loomis, who, in turn, read an address of some length, ending by transferring the remains formally to the charge of Admiral Sigsbee. Later the remains were conducted to the railway depot, placed in a car and sealed. At 9:10 that evening the car containing the body of John Paul Jones, and the American landing party as escort proceeded to Cherbourg.

Early the following morning, the 7th, the train arrived, and the remains were deposited in a pavilion to await the arrival of Admiral Sigsbee who had remained in Paris. The Admiral returned to Cherbourg early in the morning of the 8th, and at one o'clock in the afternoon the escort, which had returned from Paris to the ships on the previous day, was again landed to take part in the last ceremonies before the return voyage to the United States. These having been concluded, the casket was transferred from shore to the French torpedo boat Zouave, transported to the Brooklyn, and the American squadron then took its departure for the United States.

References: Sec. Navy An. Rep., 1878, 283; id., 1889, 824; Collum's Hist. U.S. Marine Corps, 232, 276; Log of Constitution; Marine Corps Archives; John Paul Jones, Commemoration, 101-114, Navy Library.

HAITI

(1888)

The American steamer *Haytian Republic*, sailed from the port of New York on October 4th, bound for Haiti. On the 21st of the same month she was seized by the Haitian man of war *Dessalines*, as she was leaving the Bay of St. Marc, on the charge of breach of blockade, and was taken into the port of Port au Prince. Upon arrival at the latter place, she was condemned by a special prize court, which had been convened for the purpose.

The United States objected to her seizure, and Rear Admiral Stephen B. Luce, U.S.N., was sent with the *Galena* and *Yantic* to Port au Prince to take the *Haytian Republic*, in the event the Haitian authorities refused to give her up. These two ships carried one Marine officer, First Lieutenant Benjamin R. Russell, and 45 enlisted Marines, who were at the disposal of the Admiral in carrying out his mission.

Admiral Luce arrived at Port au Prince on December 20th, informed the American Minister John E. W. Thompson of his mission, who, in turn, represented the facts to the Haitian officials, who finally agreed to release the American vessel, paying an indemnity for her arrest and detention. Force was not resorted to, but it is believed that its display contributed largely, in bringing about the desired results.

(1914)

Many revolutions, and counter revolutions, had occurred in this island republic prior to the present year, but they had not been serious enough to warrant landings or occupations by foreign governments. In the present year, however, such action became necessary.

The government headed by President Theodor had been in disfavor for some time, and conditions were such that certain European governments, considering their nationals in danger, ordered warships to Haiti for observation purposes and, if necessary, to land their Marines.

In January, the British, French and German ships lying off Port au Prince landed their Marines for the protection of their consulates. On the 29th the cruiser *South Carolina* of the American navy, arrived at this port, and landed her Marine Guard, under the command of First Lieutenant Andrew B. Drum, where they remained until the 9th of the following month. Upon the display of this force conditions became more normal, and all Marines were withdrawn, those of Great Britain, France, and Germany departing before the American Marines.

(Haiti)

(1915)

The apparent tranquility which followed the landings of the year previous was short-lived, but one year had passed when the government under President Theodor was overthrown, and, in March, succeeded by Vilbrun Guillaume Sam. The latter's regime did not appear any more popular than had that of Theodor. President Sam had not been in office more than four months when a new revolution broke out. In an apparent effort to quickly crush this outbreak, he incarcerated a large number of the politically prominent citizens of the Island, and, no doubt believing to make himself more secure, ordered the execution of the greater part of those he had put in prison.

This action had in reality the opposite effect, and the mob became so infuriated that President Sam sought refuge in the French Legation. This, however, did not save him from the vengeance of their fury. They invaded the French Legation, seized President Sam, removed him to the street, decapitated him, cut his body to pieces, placed his head on a pike, and paraded with it through the streets of the city. Naturally anarchy quickly followed.

The United States Government had been following the trend of events for some time, and had placed naval vessels in that locality to observe and report on conditions. Rear Admiral William B. Caperton, aboard the Washington, was at Cape Haitien prior to this affair, where he had landed the Marine detachment, under the command of Captain George Van Orden to quell a disturbance in that city, on the 9th of July. While proceeding to Port au Prince on the 27th he received advices from the American Minister, Mr. Arthur Bailly-Blanchard, notifying him of the serious conditions then prevailing in the capital city. In addition to the regular Marine detachment, the Washington had the 12th Company of Marines, under the command of Captain Giles Bishop, Jr., aboard. Admiral Caperton arrived at Port au Prince on the 28th of July, the day of the assassination, but not until after the assassination had been committed, and immediately landed two battalions of Marines and sailors to prevent further rioting, and for the protection of the lives of foreigners and their property. Believing his available force insufficient to cope with the conditions, the Admiral sent an urgent dispatch to the Navy Department requesting the transfer of at least a full regiment of Marines to Port au Prince as soon as possible. This received immediate response, and on the 31st, five companies of the Second Regiment under Colonel Theodore P. Kane embarked on the Connecticut, and

(Haiti)

sailed for Port au Prince. In the meantime the 24th Company of Marines under the command of Captain William G. Fay, stationed at the naval station, Guantanamo Bay, Cuba, had been transported to Haiti, and landed on the 29th.

The force was still inadequate for the duty at hand, and Admiral Caperton made a second request for Marines. This time the Headquarters, 1st Brigade, under Colonel Littleton W. T. Waller, the 1st Regiment under Colonel Eli K. Cole, and the Artillery Battalion, under Major Robert H. Dunlap, were ordered to Haiti to reinforce those preceding them to that island. The Brigade Headquarters and 1st Regiment sailed on August 10th, on the Tennessee, while the Artillery Battalion sailed on August 24th, also on the Tennessee, on her second trip to Haiti.

A new President (Dartiguenave) was elected, and installed on August 12th. One of his first duties was the negotiation of a treaty with the United States. This was prepared and signed four days later (16th), and, in general terms, provided for a Financial Adviser, Receiver of Customs, Director of Public Works and Sanitation, and a Gendarmerie, composed of native Haitians, but officered by United States Marines, who were to be commissioned as officers in that service and extra compensation from the Haitian Government. The Gendarmerie (now Garde d'Haiti) has been augmented, drilled and schooled, with native officers installed from time to time, as their training permitted, until it has become a well disciplined organization capable of maintaining peace and tranquility, if not undermined by revolutionary intrigue or civil strife.

On February 11, 1922, Brigadier General John H. Russell of the Marines (the present Major General Commandant) was appointed American High Commissioner and Personal Representative of the President of the United States, with the rank of Ambassador Extraordinary, which position he held until November 12, 1930. This is the first and only instance in history, it is believed, that an officer of the Marine Corps, or Navy, has been appointed and served in a position similar to that which General Russell occupied in Haiti.

Since their landing, on July 28, 1915, the United States Marines remained on such duty until August 15, 1934, when they were withdrawn by direction of President Franklin Delano Roosevelt.

The achievements of the Marines in Haiti, during this period of slightly over nineteen years, constitute one of the bright pages of American history. They were a people

(Haiti)

torn with revolution and misery, but now peaceful conditions reign, personal liberty, and prosperity prevail to such an extent as never known before in that country.

References: Moore's Int. Law Dig., VII, 117-118; Sec. Navy An. Rep., 1891, 617; Major-General Commandant An. Rep., 1915, 763; Log of Kearsarge; Marine Corps Archives; St. Dept. Archives.

HAWAIIAN ISLANDS

(1870)

The latter part of this year was the occasion for a pall of sadness to descend upon this group of beautiful islands - The Crossroads of the Pacific. In September the consort of King Kamehameha V., Queen Kalama, was called by death. This event engulfed the entire population in deepest mourning. Shortly before the Queen's demise, the <u>Jamestown</u>, paid a visit to Honolulu, and was there when her death occurred.

On the 21st of September all flags of foreign countries were to be placed at half-mast, in respect to the late Queen. However, the American Consul, Mr. Thomas Adamson, Jr., was of the opinion that his authority did not permit of his compliance to half-mast the American flag which flew over the Consulate, and, consequently, refused to do so. This fact came to the attention of Captain William T. Truxton of the <u>Jamestown</u>, who did not agree with the Consul's opinion, and ordered Lieutenant Henry C. Cochrane, of the Marine Guard, together with five of his men, to proceed on shore and place the American colors at half-mast, which order was promptly carried out.

(1874)

A new king was elected to the throne of these islands in February of this year, which event was the occasion for riotous proceedings, and at the pressing request of the authorities, Commander Joseph S. Skerrett of the <u>Portsmouth</u>, and Commander George E. Belknap of the <u>Tuscarora</u>, sent their Marine Guards (37 men), and a detachment of sailors ashore on the 12th to preserve order, and to protect American lives and interests. Upon arriving ashore, they occupied the court house, and posted sentries at other public buildings. No further disturbances followed, and the new king was inaugurated. On the 16th part of the landing party returned to their respective ships; leaving 19 Marines and 14 sailors until the 20th, when they also returned. There were no Marine officers aboard these two warships; their guards being in charge of Orderly Sergeants Frederick R. Mann, and Theodore Hoff, of the <u>Portsmouth</u> and <u>Tuscarora</u>, respectively.

(1889)

A revolution was in progress in this Island Kingdom, which grew to such proportions by the middle of the year as

(Hawaiian Islands)

to cause concern for the safety of foreign residents as well as foreign legations. The Adams, Commander Edwin T. Woodward, was in the harbor at Honolulu at the time. The Commander, in consultation with the American Minister, decided that a landing force was necessary for protection of American interests. Accordingly, he ordered the Marine Guard, under command of 2nd Lieutenant Charles A. Doyen, to proceed ashore to the American Legation. They landed at 10:30 a.m., July 30th, and remained until the following day.

(1893)

The ancient native kingdom was overthrown early in this year; Queen Liliuokalani deposed, and a provisional government formed, preparatory to the establishment of a republic. Because of the threatened disorder consequent to this event, it was deemed advisable to have a small American force on shore for its moral effect as well as for protection of American interests in case of necessity. The Boston, Captain Gilbert C. Wiltse, U.S. Navy, commanding, was at Honolulu at this time, and he ordered 1st Lieutenant Herbert L. Draper and his Marines ashore on January 16th to assist in maintaining order and protecting foreigners. This duty was continued until April 1st, when they returned to the Boston.

The Marines performed their duty in such an efficient manner that the Executive and Advisory Councils conveyed their appreciation and thanks to Lieutenant Draper in the form of a resolution, dated April 3rd.

References: Marine Corps Chronology; Log of Jamestown; St. Dept. Archives; Sec. Navy An. Rep., 1874, 8; Logs of Portsmouth and Tuscarora; Marine Corps Archives; Log of Adams; Collum's Hist. U.S. Marine Corps, 303; Log of Boston.

HONDURAS
(1903)

Christopher Columbus was the first European to land on the shores of Central America. On his fourth voyage to the New World in 1502, he landed at the mouth of the Segovia (Coco or Wanks) River at Cape Gracias a Dios. Twenty-two years later Cristobal de Olid, one of Cortes' lieutenants, founded the settlement of Triunfo de la Cruz. He attempted to establish an independent government, but was assassinated by an emissary of Cortes before his plans could materialize. A few years later, Honduras was joined to Guatemala as one of her provinces, and remained as such until the successful revolt against Spanish rule in 1821. Then for nearly two decades it was successively a part of Iturbide's Mexican empire and a member of the United Provinces of Central America.

On October 26, 1838, Honduras declared her complete independence, and maintained this status until the Year 1847, when she joined Nicaragua and Salvador in a loose confederation which lasted until 1863. In this year Honduras separated from this confederation and became an independent republic. This latter status continued for forty years, notwithstanding the fact that it has been the scene of frequent revolutions, alternated with corrupt dictatorships. Relatively weak, this republic has suffered the frequent interference of neighboring countries in its domestic affairs which, added to its own internal turmoils, has kept it in an almost continual state of unrest.

In this year (1903), Manuel Bonilla gained the presidency and seemed likely to repeat the success of Marco Aurelio Soto in maintaining order. However, as his term of office drew to a close, and his reelection appeared certain, the supporters of rival candidates and some of his own dissatisfied adherents intrigued to secure the cooperation of Nicaragua for his overthrow. Bonilla welcomed the opportunity which a successful campaign would assure for consolidating his own position. Jose Santos Zelaya, president of Nicaragua, was equally anxious, and several alleged violations of territory had embittered popular feeling on both sides. The United States and Mexican governments endeavored to secure a peaceful settlement without intervention, but failed.

During this period of revolutionary intrigue, the United States had several naval vessels in Honduran waters

(Honduras)

to look after American interests. These vessels were the Marietta, Lieutenant-Commander Samuel W. B. Diehl, Olympia (flagship of Rear Admiral J. B. Coghlan), Panther, Commander J. C. Wilson, Raleigh, Commander Arthur P. Nazro, and San Francisco, Captain Asa Walker. On March 15th this squadron sailed from Culebra, W.I., and arrived off the port of Puerto Cortez about the 21st. Different ships of the squadron then visited the ports of La Ceiba, Trujillo, Tela, and Puerto Sierra. Conditions at all of these ports, with the exception of Puerto Cortez, were quiet. At the latter port conditions were quite serious and at the request of the American Consul, William E. Alger, a Marine guard of 13 Marines from the Marietta was landed on the 23rd of March for the protection of the Consulate. This guard remained until the 30th or 31st, when it was withdrawn.

On the 24th of March, the flagship Olympia landed a detachment of 30 Marines, under the command of Captain Henry W. Carpenter, U.S.M.C., and Midshipman Kintner, to guard the Steamship Wharf at Puerto Cortez. They returned to the ship on the 26th.

(1907)

In February of this year a new outbreak of hostilities occurred between this republic and Nicaragua. The Honduran forces were commanded by Bonilla in person and by General Sotero Barahona, his Minister of War. One of their chief subordinates was Lee Christmas, an adventurer from Memphis, Tenn., who had previously been a locomotive-driver. Honduras received active support from its ally, Salvador, and was favored by public opinion throughout Central America. But from the outset the Nicaraguans proved victorious, largely owing to their mobility. Their superior naval force enabled them to capture Puerto Cortez and La Ceiba, and to threaten other cities on the Caribbean Coast; on land they were aided by a body of Honduran rebels, who also established a provisional government. Zelaya captured Tegucigalpa after severe fighting, and besieged Bonilla in Amapala. Lee Christmas was killed. The surrender of Amapala on the 11th of April practically ended the war, and Bonilla took refuge on board the United States cruiser Chicago. A noteworthy feature of the war was the attitude of the American naval officers, who landed Marines, arranged the surrender of Amapala, and prevented Nicaragua prolonging hostilities. Honduras was now evacuated by the Nicaraguans and her provisional government was recognized by Zelaya.

Commander Albert G. Winterhalter, in the Paducah, was looking after American interests in the vicinity of Puerto Cortez. Due to the serious state of affairs around Laguna and Choloma (on the Chamelicon River), he deemed it necessary to land his Marine Guard for their protection.

(Honduras)

Accordingly, the entire guard of 12 Marines, under the command of Ensign Lawrence P. Treadwell, were landed at Laguna on the 28th of April, and remained there until the 23rd of May. On this date they were transferred to Choloma, where they guarded American interests until the 8th of June.

(1924)

Political conditions in this republic had remained peaceful for nearly seventeen years, until this year when there was an outbreak of hostilities over the selection or election of a president. During the latter part of February and until the latter part of April these disturbances were at their height, and considerable fear was entertained for the safety of foreigners - especially around La Ceiba, Puerto Cortez and Tela.

Rear Admiral John H. Dayton, commander of the Special Service Squadron, in the flagship Rochester, proceeded to Honduran waters late in the previous year, and was present when the outbreak of hostilities occurred. The Admiral was now aboard the Denver and, on the 27th of February that ship anchored off La Ceiba. Early in the morning of the 28th, he went ashore to gain all information possible from the American Consul, George P. Waller, relative to local conditions. He found that a battle between the revolutionists and government troops was imminent, and deemed that a landing force of Marines and sailors was necessary for the protection of American interests. Returning to the Denver he ordered the Marine detachment, consisting of First Lieutenant Theodore H. Cartwright and 46 enlisted men, together with a detachment of bluejackets, the whole under the command of the Marine lieutenant, to be despatched ashore to protect the American Consulate. The expected battle took place early the following morning, the 29th.

The Denver remained at this port until the 2nd of March, when she proceeded to Tela. The following day she sailed for Puerto Cortez, arriving in the forenoon of the same day. The Marine detachment of the Florida under the command of Captain Robert L. Nelson and First Lieutenant Charles H. Hassenmiller had been previously transferred to the Billingsley and Lardner, as was also the Fleet Marine officer, Major Edward W. Sturdevant. On the 3rd of March the Billingsley put in to La Ceiba and embarked the landing force from the Denver, and transported them to that vessel, which was then anchored at Puerto Cortez. One first sergeant and 10 enlisted Marines were retained on the Billingsley, and she sailed the same day for Tela. At 9 o'clock the same evening these Marines, under the command of Lieutenant Vincent H. Godfrey, U.S.N., together with a number of sailors,

(Honduras)

were landed to protect American citizens. This force remained on shore until the morning of the 13th, when they were withdrawn to their ship.

On March 8th, the Lardner came to anchor off La Ceiba, and her commander, Lieutenant Commander Frank E. P. Uberroth, found that the withdrawal of the landing force of the Denver, (landed on February 28th and withdrawn on March 3rd), had been inopportune, for he had no more than anchored before the American Consul, Mr. Waller, requested that another force be landed for the protection of American citizens. Captain Nelson, of the Marines, 40 enlisted Marines and 45 sailors were immediately despatched on shore in accordance with the Consul's desires, and they remained until the afternoon of the 13th, when they returned to the ship.

While these landings at La Ceiba and Tela were taking place, other landings were also being made. As stated before, the Denver arrived at Puerto Cortez early in the morning of March 3rd. Upon arrival here Admiral Dayton conferred with the American Consul, George P. Shaw, the result of which was the decision to establish a neutral zone and despatch a landing force to maintain compliance with the rules laid down for its enforcement, and protect foreigners within this zone. A force of 8 officers and 159 Marines and sailors, under the command of Major Sturdevant, of the Marines, was accordingly landed at 4:40 p.m. of the 4th. This landing party returned to the ship about mid-afternoon of the 6th. During the time they were ashore, they disarmed some of the de facto Government troops, and sent their arms, including one field piece, two machine guns, twenty-three rifles besides a quantity of assorted ammunition, aboard the Denver. These were returned to the shore the following morning, and placed in custody of Major Sturdevant.

On the morning of the 8th, the Denver proceeded to Tela and anchored off that port. The same afternoon a landing force of 5 officers and 65 Marines and sailors, under the command of Major Sturdevant, were despatched ashore to augment the force from the Billingsley (previously mentioned), and remained on this duty until the morning of the 9th, when they were withdrawn and the Denver sailed for La Ceiba. She arrived at the latter port the same afternoon, and immediately landed Major Sturdevant, two other officers and 21 Marines. They remained ashore until the 13th.

No further landings were necessary for the protection of American interests until the fore part of September, when the Rochester sent an armed party ashore at La Ceiba. This vessel had recently returned from the United States, and Admiral Dayton transferred his flag from the Denver to her

(Honduras)

shortly after her arrival. The Rochester came to anchor off La Ceiba on the 7th, and Admiral Dayton and the American Consul, Mr. Waller, conferred relative to the need of an armed force to protect American interests. Apparently it was agreed that such was required, for on the 10th, a force of 3 officers and 108 Marines and sailors, under the command of Captain James M. Bain, U.S.M.C., was despatched ashore and so remained until noon of the 15th, when it was returned to the ship.

(1925)

In April of this year, Honduras was the scene of another political upheaval. Although the state of affairs was not of so serious a nature as those of the previous year, the American Consul, George P. Waller, and Captain William N. Jeffers, of the Denver, considered that the presence of an armed force was necessary for the protection of foreigners at La Ceiba.

The Denver had arrived at La Ceiba on the 19th of April and, on the following day, the Marines, under First Lieutenant Theodore H. Cartwright, were despatched on shore, remaining until about noon the 21st.

References: Mov. Vessels, July 1897-June 1916, 540; Sec. Navy An. Rep., 1903, 633; id., 1924, 10, 48; id., 1925, 8; Marine Corps Archives; Logs of Marietta, Olympia, Panther, Raleigh, San Francisco, Paducah, Rochester, Denver, Billingsley, and Lardner.

JAPANESE EMPIRE
(1853)

For several years the American government had endeavored to break down the barriers the Dai-Nippon Empire had maintained against foreign governments in commercial pursuits, but all such efforts were of no avail. Commodore Biddle came the nearest to success of any of the representatives despatched from the United States when he paid a visit there in July, 1846. To all of his diplomacy, however, they still remained adamant as regards the making of any treaty with Christian nations which would open their ports to commerce.

The fact that the Japanese remained obdurate to all advances did not deter the American government in prosecuting the issue at every opportunity which presented itself. In furtherance of this idea, President Fillmore, early in 1851, commissioned Commodore John H. Aulick an envoy, with powers to negotiate a treaty. He started on this mission, but was later recalled and Commodore M. C. Perry was substituted for its completion. Perry's squadron consisted of the Mississippi, Vermont, Vandalia, Allegheny, Macedonian, Powhatan, and Southampton. The Plymouth, Saratoga and Susquehanna, taken by Commodore Aulick, were to join Perry when he arrived in Asiatic waters.

Considerable time was necessary to outfit so large a squadron, and to assemble it at a base from which to commence the operations necessitated by his mission. He selected Shanghai as his place of rendezvous, and about the middle of May (1853), had everything in readiness for the actual start of the treaty mission. On the 23rd the squadron sailed for the Lew Chew Islands, arriving three days later at the port of Napha, where the Commodore was received by the Regent, and lavishly entertained. On his visit, the Commodore was escorted by a force of Marines and sailors from his ships.

On July 2nd Perry sailed from Napha for Uraga, Japan, arriving six days later. On the 13th the Governor visited the Commodore, at which time arrangements were completed for a landing of the Americans on the following day. This plan was accomplished without mishap, and Perry landed with a force of nearly 300 officers, Marines and sailors. Major Jacob Zeilin commanded the Marines, and was the second person to set foot on Japanese soil. Prince Toda and Prince Ido received the Commodore, to whom he presented President Fillmore's letter. His reception was anything but cordial and, he was informed in substance, that as the letter had been received, he, Perry, could depart. To this the Commo-

(Japanese Empire)

dore informed them that he would depart for the Lew Chew Islands, and that they could communicate with him there. He also advised that he would return to Japan the following spring.

The squadron finally returned to Shanghai, its place of rendezvous, and while here (in November), the Commodore became suspicious when the French frigate Constantine hurriedly left Macao under sealed orders, and a Russian squadron (which had lately visited Nagasaki), arrived at Shanghai. He thought it quite possible that they might proceed to Japan and ruin his plans. He decided to move at once, and was prepared to sail when he received orders to detach one of his vessels and place it at the disposal of the recently appointed commissioner to China, Robert M. McLane. As this would thwart his previous plans, he decided to wait until after his demonstration in Yedo Bay before carrying out this order.

(1854)

The Commodore sailed with his squadron on January 14th for the Lew Chew Islands, where he arrived on the 20th. While at this port he despatched the Lexington, Macedonian, Southampton and Vandalia to the Bay of Yedo and followed them with the Mississippi, Powhatan, Saratoga, and Susquehanna, on the 7th of February. Four days later he arrived off the Bay of Yedo, but encountered a severe storm, and could not bring his ships to anchor near Uraga until the 13th. After the squadron came to anchor two minor officials appeared with a message from the Emperor. Proposals and counter proposals were exchanged until the 25th, when it was agreed that March 8th should be the day of meeting for treaty conversations. In the meantime Perry had changed the position of his vessels; had transferred his flag to the Powhatan, and had brought her opposite the village of Yokuhama (Yokohama), where he could see Yedo from his masthead.

Commodore Perry ordered "all the Marines of the squadron, who can be spared from duty," as well as a considerable force of sailors, to act as his escort ashore. This force numbered approximately 500 officers and men, and required 27 boats to transport them to the landing place. The escort preceded the Commodore ashore, and when he arrived he was

(Japanese Empire)

received with somewhat pompous ceremonies which seemed to impress the Japanese considerably. The Japanese commissioners were awaiting his arrival and after the ceremonies were over, the conference was begun. One of the first subjects discussed was to effect arrangements for interring the body of a Marine (Private Williams), who had died two days before on the Mississippi.

At first the Commissioners stated that it was impossible to permit the burial on Japanese soil. However, after considerable "palaver" they finally consented and the interment took place at, or near, the village of Yokohama on the following day, March 9th. The conference for the day having been concluded, Perry, his officers, and his escort returned to their respective ships.

About three in the afternoon of the following day the body escort, firing party and others who were to attend the funeral left the ship for the landing place. They were met by the Mayor of Uraga who conducted them through the village to a wooded hill near a temple, the site selected for the interment. The body was laid to rest with the customary rites. (Incidentally, this was the first American military man buried in Japanese soil). After the American rites were concluded, a Japanese Buddhist priest performed the Japanese ceremonies for the dead over this Marine's grave.

Guarded by a company of Marines, presents were despatched to the Emperor by the Commodore on March 13th. Japanese officials received these, and directed their disposition to the locations where the Americans were to give demonstrations as to their use. At this same time another meeting was arranged between Perry and the Commissioners to take place on the 17th. At this conference Perry was promised a reply from the Emperor on the 24th, relative to concluding a treaty which promise was kept, and was followed by presents from the Emperor.

The negotiations were followed by the signing of a treaty of "Peace, Commerce, and Navigation" on the 31st of March, 1854, which event was celebrated by a dinner ashore. Perry had succeeded where many others had failed! This treaty opened two ports to commerce, Shimoda and Hakodate, and provided for the exchange of ratifications within eighteen months from date of effectiveness. Commander Henry A. Adams, U.S. Navy, was designated "bearer of the treaty" to the

(Japanese Empire)

United States. He sailed aboard the Saratoga on the 4th of April, reached the Hawaiian Islands on the 29th, transferred to a "more speedy conveyance," and reached Washington on the 10th of July.

So arduous had been the efforts of the Commodore in effecting this treaty that his health was impaired and he asked to be sent home to recuperate. This request was granted, and in the latter part of July he turned over his command, having successfully concluded his mission, took passage on the English mail steamer Hindostan, and arrived at the port of New York on January 12, 1855.

(1860)

In this year Japan sent to the United States the first Embassy that had ever gone to a foreign country. The Empire not having a vessel suitable to make such a long journey, requested the American Minister to permit them to proceed on one of the United States men-of-war. This request was granted, and the Powhatan was selected for the mission and sailed from Yedo on February 13th. Captain Algernon S. Taylor, of the Marines, was detailed to accompany them, and look out for their welfare and comfort on the trip. They arrived at Washington on the 14th of May.

(1863)

In June of this year, the American steamer Pembroke was making passage from Yokohama to Nagasaki, and while passing through the straits of Shimonoseki was fired upon by shore batteries and by an armed brig belonging to the Prince of Nagato. She was not struck, but discontinued her voyage and returned to Nagasaki. The American Minister demanded redress for the insult to the American flag, and by his direction Commander McDougall, of the Wyoming, with a Marine detachment, proceeded on July 13th to retaliate upon the hostile daimio. He arrived there on the 16th, found three vessels belonging to the Prince, attacked them, and after a sharp conflict with them and the shore batteries, sank a brig and blew up a steamer, by which action some 40 persons were said to have been killed. The Wyoming lost 5 killed and 6 wounded.

(Japanese Empire)

(1867)

During the early part of this year, the Tycoon invited the foreign ministers resident in Japan to his country residence for an interview. The American Minister, Mr. Van Valkenburgh, requested Rear Admiral Bell to accompany him on the visit. To this the Admiral readily assented, and deemed that the Minister should be conveyed there in his flagship, the Hartford, accompanied by two other vessels of his squadron, the Shenandoah and Wyoming. The Hartford, however, was disabled, but the Minister was accommodated on the Shenandoah, and together with the Wyoming, they proceeded and landed on the 1st of May at Osaka with the usual honors, and escorted by the Marine Guard of both vessels.

(1868)

The civil war in Japan, over the abolition of the Shogunate and restoration of the Mikado, coupled with the events of the opening of the ports of Osaka and Hiogo, made it necessary to land Marines on several occasions during this year for the protection of American lives and property. Difficulties originating in the innovations on ancient customs, and opposition to intercourse with foreigners, appeared among the Japanese, and soon developed into hostilities. On the 27th of January the contending parties came into conflict at Osaka. The Tycoon was defeated, and during the night of the 31st sought refuge, with some of his adherents, on board the Iroquois, which was then lying in th harbor. Shelter was afforded him until the next morning (February 1st), when he was transferred to one of his own vessels of war.

On the First of February, several foreign ministers who were compelled to abandon Osaka, were received on board the Iroquois, and conveyed to Hiogo. The Fourth of the same month an assault was made on foreign residents by a detachment of Japanese troops, during which one of the crew of the Oneida was seriously wounded. Due to this outbreak the naval forces present made a joint landing, and adopted measures to protect the foreign settlement. These forces, including American Marines and sailors, remained ashore until February 8th. On this latter date a messenger arrived from the Mikado with information of a change of government, and assurances that foreigners would be protected. The Japanese officer who was responsible for this assault was subsequently

(Japanese Empire) 104

executed in the presence of a number of officers of the vessels of war then present in the harbor of Hiogo. On this same date (February 8th), the American Consul at Nagasaki, Mr. Moore, requested the commander of the Shenandoah to land a force of Marines and sailors for the protection of the Consulate. This request was granted.

On the Third of April, the naval commanders then present at Yokohama representing France, England, Italy, Prussia and the United States, pursuant to a request of the diplomatic officials of their respective countries, held a conference to decide upon ways and means for the protection of their interests, and the foreign settlement in general. The decision reached was that each naval commander should land a certain force; the whole to be disposed as suggested by the American Minister, Mr. Van Valkenburgh. This decision was placed in operation, and a landing force of 25 American Marines from the Monocacy and Iroquois were ashore from the 4th of April to the 12th of May. Lieutenant G.D.B. Glidden, of the U.S. Navy, commanded the Marines on this occasion. A month later (June 12th) while the Iroquois was anchored in the harbor of Yokohama it was perceived that the Japanese ship Kaugi No Kami was preparing to leave the harbor in violation of the neutrality law. An officer and three Marines from the Iroquois were despatched to board and prevent her departure. On June 13, this duty having been performed they returned aboard their ship.

A Marine Guard was maintained at the American Minister's residence from January 19th and, on September 25th, the Minister stated: "A guard of Marines * * * is still stationed on shore." The log of the Piscataqua shows that Second Lieutenant John C. Morgan, U.S.M.C., and 4 Marines returned from the American Minister's on the 26th of September.

(1890)

Rear Admiral George E. Belknap, commander-in-chief of the Asiatic fleet, in his flagship Omaha, paid a visit to Yokohama in the latter part of the preceding year. During his stay at this port an extensive conflagration occurred in the native town of Hodogaya, a suburb of Kanagawa, on the night of February 8th. The disaster was so serious that the United States Consul General, Mr. Clarence R. Greathouse, requested Admiral Belknap to land a force from his ship to give assistance to the local authorities in subduing the flames. This request met with instant compliance on the

(Japanese Empire)

part of the Admiral, who despatched a large party ashore for the purpose. The Marines, under the command of First Lieutenant William C. Turner, U.S.M.C., assisted, as a part of the landing party. The Governor of Kanagawa cordially acknowledged the assistance given by the force from the Omaha.

References: McClellan's Hist. U.S. Marine Corps; Moore's Int. Law Dig., VII, 116; Collum's Hist. U.S. Marine Corps; Marine Corps Muster Rolls, Marine Corps Archives; Hawk's Japan Exped; Dip. Corr., I, 707, 824; Logs of Powhatan, Wyoming, Oneida, Piscataqua, Monocacy, Iroquois and Omaha; Sec. Navy An. Rep., 1887, 5; id., 1890, 134.

JOHANNA ISLAND

(1851)

The captain of the whaling brig Maria, Captain Charles C. Moores of Nantucket, was unlawfully imprisoned by King Selim of this island. In August of this year, the U. S. sloop Dale, under the command of Commander William Pearson, was in this vicinity on a regular cruise of the southern Pacific islands. Information of this outrage was communicated to Commander Pearson. He proceeded to the Island for the purpose of exacting redress. Arriving there about the 5th of August, he communicated his demands to the authorities. On the morning of the 6th, Mr. Martindale, an English merchant of the town, repaired on board the Dale with a message from the King, in which he refused to comply with the demands made by Commander Pearson.

Upon receiving this refusal, the Dale's commander, no doubt, felt that a few round shot was necessary to bring the obdurate monarch to terms. Combining action with the thought, at 9:06 a.m., he directed fire be opened upon the fort on shore from his port battery. After the firing of six guns, a white flag was seen flying over the shore fortifications. All firing was stopped, and a boat carrying Acting Lieutenant Reginald Fairfax, was despatched ashore to confer with the authorities. Lieutenant Fairfax soon returned, but with little success for his trip, for the King still refused compliance with previous demands for redress.

Commander Pearson then ordered the boat to return ashore and inform the authorities to haul down the white flag, as he intended to reopen fire on the fort. This message was delivered, the boat returned, and at 11:05 a.m., the guns of the Dale opened a second time on the fort and bastion at the extreme left of the town. Twenty-six round shot and four shell were fired at the fort, and nine round shot at the bastion. At 11:50 all firing ceased, and, at 1:00 p.m., Lieutenant Parker, accompanied by Mr. Martindale, went ashore to learn if the authorities were now ready to meet the terms of Commander Pearson.

The chastisement administered by the sloop had immediate results for the boat, it seemed, had hardly left the ship's side before it was back, carrying the King's Treasurer and an attendant. On the following day, the 7th, the Treasurer again repaired aboard "with a quantity of money." (According to a letter of the U. S. State Department, dated December 17, 1852, the amount was $1,000.00).

While the sloop Dale was anchored off this island an

(Johanna Island)

incident took place, not connected with the original mission, but, nevertheless, one well worth recording as an indication of the watchfulness of Commander Pearson over the interests of the American people, and the varied duties to which the Marines are called upon to perform.

The American bark *Paulina* was at anchor in the harbor at the same time as the *Dale* and, on the morning of August 9th, hoisted the American flag, union down. Commander Pearson realized that something was amiss so he despatched two boats with officers and Marines to board her and learn the cause. This party boarded the *Paulina*, found a portion of her crew were about to mutiny, placed them in confinement, and departed, with the admonition that a repetition would bring forth severe action.

On August 29th, all difficulties having been settled, the sloop saluted the Flag of King Selim with 21 guns and, on September 1st, weighed anchor and sailed out of the harbor.

References: Log of *Dale*; Moore's Int. Law Dig., VII, 112; Dom. Let. vol. 41, 1852 to Sept. 1853, 150-151; Marine Corps Archives.

LUCHU ISLANDS*

(1853)

Chinese invasions of these islands may be traced back to the year 605 A.D., but they did not result in annexation, and it was not until 1372 that China obtained from the Luchuans recognition of supremacy. Luchuan relations with Japan had long been friendly, but at the end of the 16th century the king (regent) refused Japan assistance against Corea (now Chosen), and in 1609 the prince Satsuma invaded the islands with 3000 men, took the capital by storm, captured the king and carried him off to Kagoshima. A few years later he was restored to his throne on condition of acknowledging Japanese suzerainty, and the payment of tribute. Notwithstanding this agreement with the Japanese, the Luchuans continued to pay tribute to China also. The islanders were now in the impossible position of attempting to serve two masters.

Commodore Matthew C. Perry was conversant with the affairs of the Luchu Regency, and considered it worth while to pay a visit to the islands to establish friendly relations with the people and possibly negotiate a treaty with the regent. Accordingly, when he sailed from Shanghai for Japan in May of this year, he stopped at the Luchu Islands in furtherance of this plan. Perry's squadron arrived at the port of Napa (Nafa) about the 26th, and the Regent paid a visit to the flagship four days later, which Perry returned on the 6th of June. It was the Commodore's desire to visit the Regent at his palace, but the Luchuans apparently did not wish it so, and practiced every subterfuge known by them to inveigle Perry into changing his plans. However, Perry was not to be so persuaded. He persevered in his original intention, and finally won his point to visit the Regent at his palace.

Knowing the characteristics of the oriental race, Perry decided to make his visit to the Regent an elaborate ceremony - one to make a lasting impression on the people of the island. And to carry out this idea he had detailed the entire Marine guard of the <u>Mississippi</u> and <u>Susquehanna</u>, in full dress uniform, under Major Jacob Zeilin, together with the band of each ship and officers and sailors to a total of nearly 300, and not forgetting two brass field pieces with their crews of sailors to add to the attraction, landed the

---

* Several different spellings of the name of these islands have been used by writers of history and in official records of the Navy Department, such as: Loo Choo, Lew Chew, Luchu, Loochoo, Liukiu, and Riu Kiu. These islands came under Japanese control in 1879.

whole force at the village of Tumai, about two miles from the Palace of Shui. Perry, himself, waited until the landing party had reached shore before he left the ship. When the landing party had been arranged for Perry's reception, he proceeded to the landing place, and the procession was formed for the march to the Palace. Upon arrival there, Perry was the first American naval officer to be received by the Regent. A grand entertainment was held, very cordial relations established, and Perry with his escort returned to the ships of the squadron early in the afternoon.

Commodore Perry remained at this port until the 2nd of July before continuing on to Japan. On the 28th of June, the Regent and the Treasurer of Luchu were invited aboard Perry's flagship, the Susquehanna, to dine, and be entertained.

On the 23rd of July, Perry with his squadron returned to Luchu on his way from Japan to his rendezvous at Shanghai, and on the 28th attended a dinner given by the Regent to the officers of the American vessels. While here, the Commodore arranged for the rental of a coaling station for his ships, in order that they might be refueled without having to proceed to China or other place for the necessary coal. This mission having been concluded, the squadron sailed for its base of operations on the 1st of August, leaving Commander John Kelly, and the Plymouth behind to keep alive the friendly relations established.

(1854)

Perry's third visit to the Luchu Islands was on his return from his second voyage to Japan. He arrived at the port of Napa on the 1st of July, and there learned of the murder of William Boardman and the injuries to another man named Scott, of the Lexington, which occurred on the 19th of the previous month at the market place in Napa. The Commodore, finding that the authorities were inclined to procrastination instead of a prompt settlement of the affair, believed that an armed demonstration might influence them in expediting the matter. He waited, however, until the 6th before carrying out this plan. Not having received proper redress in the meantime, Captain Robert Tansill, commanding the Marines of the Powhatan, was ordered to select 20 of his men, proceed ashore and take possession of the Temple and Yard at Tumai, allowing no native to enter or remain within the precincts. The Regent was then advised that the Marines had been landed. This information had the desired result, for early the following day, the 7th, the affair was settled to the satisfaction of all concerned.

The negotiation of a treaty with the Luchu regent had

(Luchu Islands)

not been forgotten by Perry - he was simply waiting for an opportune occasion to begin conversations on the subject. The Boardman affair having been amicably concluded, Perry believed that the time was now ripe to commence the treaty negotiations. On the 11th, he ordered an escort of Marines to be made ready to accompany him, and about noon left the ship for shore. Arriving there, accompanied by his escort of Marines, he proceeded to the Town Hall, found the Regent awaiting him, and the conversations began. After some little time devoted to the subject of the treaty, a compact or treaty was signed by the Regent, and the occasion was celebrated by "a handsome entertainment, furnished by the Lew Chew authorities." On the 14th, Perry gave a parting entertainment aboard his ship, and on the 17th sailed for Hong Kong.

The next American naval vessel to visit these islands was the <u>Vincennes</u>, under the command of Lieutenant John Rodgers, and her Marine guard in charge of Orderly Sergeant James McDonough. This ship arrived at Napa on the 16th of November, 1854. Lieutenant Rodgers desired to purchase firewood, and other articles for his vessel, but since the Luchuans did not seem disposed to accommodate him, he then requested an audience with the Regent, which was granted. It was arranged to hold this in the Court House at Napa. Lieutenant Rodgers, accompanied by as many officers as could be spared, together with an escort of the Marines, repaired to the place of meeting, where he found the Regent waiting. The results of this audience were unsatisfactory - it appearing that the Regent was not inclined to observe the terms of Perry's Treaty, and that his whole attitude was one of manifest evasion. Further conversation appeared useless, so Rodgers issued an ultimatum to the effect that, "if the wood was not furnished in twenty-four hours (he) should take an armed force with a field piece up to the Palace and learn from the Regent why he infringed" the Convention of Commodore Perry.

However, the wood was not forthcoming, and little or no attention was given to the threat issued by Lieutenant Rodgers. To this apparent defy, Rodgers replied by landing at the head of about 100 officers, Marines and sailors, all well armed, and with a field-piece marched up to the Palace at Shui. Upon arrival, he found that the Regent was absent, but was informed that the person next in rank to the Regent was present, as was also the governor of Napa, and that they would receive the Lieutenant. Rodgers agreed to this, and received a promise that the wood would be furnished without delay, as well as other concessions. Tea was now served and an entertainment furnished for Rodgers and his officers. About sunset Rodgers and his armed party returned to the ship.

(Luchu Islands)

References: McClellan's Hist. U.S. Marine Corps; Logs of
    <u>Mississippi</u>, <u>Susquehanna</u>, <u>Plymouth</u> and <u>Vincennes</u>; Marine
    Corps Archives; Navy Archives.

MARQUESAS ISLANDS

(1813)

Captain David Porter was cruising in the South Pacific during this year in search of enemy English vessels. Several had been captured and taken to the Island of Nookaheevah. Captain Porter had with him a young Marine officer, First Lieutenant John M. Gamble, under whom he placed the prizes which had been captured. Lieutenant Gamble was left at this island pending the return of Porter from another short cruise in the vicinity.

The prizes left under Lieutenant Gamble's command consisted of the Greenwich, Sir Andrew Hammond and Seringapatam. On December 9th, shortly before Porter left the Island, a fort was constructed upon a small hill, and the prizes were warped in close under its guns for their better protection. Gamble had as his force one midshipman and some 20 odd Marines and sailors, who had volunteered to remain with him until Porter's return.

Within a short time after the Essex (Porter's ship) departed, the natives of the island became very hostile in their actions toward Lieutenant Gamble. Chief Gattenewa was quite friendly, but his influence was inadequate to restrain the members of his tribe, and it became necessary for Lieutenant Gamble to land a part of his force and, by a show of arms, intimidate them, and regain the property they had pilfered from the encampment. This seemed to have the desired effect, for the Americans lived in perfect amity with the natives until May of the following year.

(1814)

In the early part of April Lieutenant Gamble having despaired of Captain Porter's return, commenced rigging two of the prizes, the Hammond and Seringapatam, preparatory to sailing for Valparaiso as had been earlier agreed to with Porter. Clear sailing was not, however, to be the lot of this intrepid young Marine officer, who had actually commanded the Greenwich during her engagement with, and capture of the Seringapatam late in the previous year.

On May 7th, a mutiny occurred on the Seringapatam, Lieutenant Gamble was wounded, and the mutineers sailed out of the bay in the ship. Two days later the few Americans that remained, were attacked by the natives and Midshipman William Felters and three men were massacred, and one of the Marines dangerously wounded. This left Lieutenant Gamble with 1 midshipman, 3 Marines, 1 seaman and 2

(Marquesas Islands)

ordinary seamen to sail the Hammond, when she was ready to put to sea, only two of whom were really fit for duty, because of wounds, illness, etc. Notwithstanding all these handicaps, Lieutenant Gamble and his small party were undaunted, and they redoubled their efforts to rig the Hammond for sea. She was finally ready to sail and, on May 9th, Gamble having ordered the one remaining prize, the Greenwich, burned, the Hammond sailed from the harbor where the Americans had suffered so many hardships.

The Hammond reached the Yahoo Islands on the 31st, secured a crew of natives, and sailed from there June 11th, only to be captured by the British ship Cherub the second day out. Finally, after about nine months had elapsed, they arrived at Rio de Janeiro, where the Americans were set at liberty. In the following year (1815), Lieutenant Gamble secured passage from Rio on a Swedish vessel bound for Havre de Grace and while enroute fell in with the American ship Oliver Ellsworth, on August 1st, bound for New York, transhipped to her, and arrived in his native land the latter part of the same month.

Commodore Porter felt so well disposed toward Lieutenant Gamble that he wrote the Secretary of the Navy: "* * * I now avail myself of the opportunity of assuring you that no Marine officer in the service ever had such strong claims as Captain Gamble, and that none have been placed in such conspicuous and critical positions, and that none could have extricated themselves from them more to their honor."

References: Collum's Hist. U.S. Marine Corps, 52-53; McClellan's Hist. U.S. Marine Corps.

MEXICO
(1870)

The merchant ship *Forward*, formerly a British gunboat, was ostensibly employed in the fishing trade on the coast of Mexico, when she was seized by an armed party acting, supposedly, under orders of Pacido Vega (a former governor of Sinaloa), in the latter part of May of this year. They raised the Salvadoran flag and, on the night of May 27th, made a raid upon Guaymas, took possession of and robbed the custom-house, forced the foreign merchants to contribute funds to a large amount, and, finally, compelled the United States Consul, over his protest, to supply coal for the vessel.

Commander William W. Low, U.S.N., with the *Mohican*, was in the vicinity, and a few days after the *Forward* was seized, paid a visit to the neighboring port of Mazatlan. While at this port, on June 6th, the American Consul, Isaac Sisson, acquainted him with the facts of the seizure, and subsequent actions of the pirate crew of the *Forward*. It was rumored that she was still in the Gulf, so Commander Low decided to locate her if possible, and exact proper redress for the outrage at Guaymas. He sailed forthwith, and proceeded along the coast for several days without learning of her whereabouts. On the morning of the 16th he reached San Blas, and despatched an officer ashore for information that might lead to her location. The officer returned and reported that the *Forward* had gone to Boca Teacapan for the purpose of landing her plunder. The Commander decided to proceed immediately in pursuit. The next morning (17th), he arrived off Boca Teacapan, ordered a landing force of Marines and sailors, under Lieutenant Willard H. Brownson, U.S.N., embarked in six boats, and despatched them up the river with instructions to find the piratical steamer and bring her out. The landing party saw nothing of the steamer, nor did they hear of her, until they had proceeded up the river about 25 miles, when they fell in with a fisherman who informed them that the *Forward* was aground some 15 miles farther up the stream. They pushed on as rapidly as possible, and, at 7:45 in the evening, sighted their quest about 200 yards off, aground, and heading inshore.

Lieutenant Brownson and his party pulled alongside, gained the decks without opposition, took possession of the vessel, and made prisoners of the six men who were on board. As the American landing party was approaching the ship, a boat was seen leaving the port bow. Ensign Wainwright being under orders to intercept and cut her off, if possible, capture her occupants, and bring them aboard the vessel, ordered a shot fired to stop the escaping boat when, almost immediately, a volley of musketry, canister and grape was fired from shore, which raked the decks and sides of the steamer, and

(Mexico)

the boat in which he was pursuing the fugitives. This volley was so severe that he had to fall back to the steamer for protection, with casualties of one killed; Assistant Engineer Townrow, two men, and himself wounded. One of the two men wounded was Private James Higgins, of the Marines.

The pirates had landed about 170 men (most of their crew) their battery of four 12-pounders, had flanked these by riflemen, and placed the whole in such a position as to bring a cross and raking fire upon the sides and decks of the grounded ship. Lieutenant Brownson, after holding the vessel for about an hour, decided that it was impossible to get her out and down the river because of the falling tide, and the manner in which she was grounded, so he then made preparations to destroy her. Placing his dead and wounded, the prisoners and most of her men in the boats, he with the few remaining fired the vessel in the coal-bunker and several places aft. As the party shoved off, they gave a parting shot of shrapnel "between wind and water" to insure her complete destruction.

The landing party pulled down the river, and regained their own ship early in the afternoon of the 18th, after having been absent about 32 hours. Lieutenant Brownson commended the officers and men of his party for their coolness and courage under most trying circumstances, and picked out several for special consideration, among whom were two Marines - First Sergeant Philip Moore and Corporal F. Moulton.

A short time after the Forward had been destroyed, Rear Admiral Thomas Turner, commander of the Pacific Fleet, paid his respects to Admiral Farquhar, of the British naval forces in the Pacific, and when about to depart from the British Flagship, Admiral Farquhar stated, apropos the Forward affair: "This is always the way with you American officers; you are ahead of us when a ship of war is required to be on the spot."

(1913)

During this year considerable fighting between different factions in Mexico was in progress, and American citizens were urged to leave the troubled area and return to the United States. Some had heeded this warning, but others had remained with their property until conditions made it necessary for United States naval forces to proceed there and assist them in making their departure.

On September 4th, Rear Admiral W. C. Cowles, commander-in-chief of the Pacific Fleet, directed Commander D. W. Blamer

(Mexico)

of the Buffalo which was at Guaymas, to proceed to Ciaris Estero, and there land Mr. R.W. Vail, American Consular Agent at Guaymas, who would proceed to the Richardson Construction Company's Headquarters in the Yaqui Valley for the purpose of bringing to the coast all Americans and foreigners who wished to avail themselves of an opportunity to leave the country, and to then sail for San Diego and land the refugees.

The Buffalo arrived at Ciaris Estero the following morning, and at 9:05 Mr. Vail, First Lieutenant John R. Henley, U.S. Marine Corps, Ensigns Hawley and Neilson, and Pilot Ross, landed and proceeded to the Yaqui Valley. This party returned on the 7th, bringing with them 12 American refugees, and 83 others from the Richardson Construction Company, who wished to leave the country. On the 14th, the Buffalo proceeded to San Diego, California where the refugees were landed.

(1914)

The culmination of indignities upon the United States by General Huerta in Mexico came in the arrest of the paymaster and boat's crew of the Dolphin at Tampico on April 6th. This ship carried, both at her bow and stern, the American flag. Admiral Mayo, who was at Tampico at the time, regarded this incident as so serious an affront as to warrant the demand that the flag of the United States by saluted with special ceremony by the military commander of the port. A few days after this incident, an orderly from the Minnesota, then at Vera Cruz, was arrested while on shore to obtain the ship's mail, and was for a time in jail. An official despatch from the American Government to its embassy in Mexico City was withheld by the authorities of the telegraphic service until peremptorily demanded by the chargé d'affaires of the United States in person. President Wilson, in his special message to Congress, on April 20th, said: "* * * I therefore felt it my duty to sustain Admiral Mayo in the whole of his demand and to insist that the flag of the United States should be saluted in such a way as to indicate a new spirit and attitude on the part of the Huertaistas. Such a salute General Huerta has refused." The President asked and obtained the approval of Congress to use the armed forces "in such ways and to such extent as may be necessary to obtain from General Huerta and his adherents the fullest recognition of the rights and dignity of the United States."

Before the fleet under Rear Admiral Badger reached the Mexican shores, it became necessary to issue orders to Rear Admiral Fletcher to seize the port of Vera Cruz. Accordingly, early in the morning of the 21st of April, Fletcher

(Mexico)

prepared a landing force of Marines and sailors from his division, constituting approximately 700 of the former and 5000 of the latter, all under the command of Captain W. R. Rush, U.S. Navy, sent them ashore in ships' boats, and the capture of the city was in progress of accomplishment. They took possession of the custom-house under a rain of fire from "snipers" hidden in every conceivable place, then proceeded in small parties to take other parts of the city, and to "mop up" the hiding places of the troublesome sharpshooters. Most of the Huerta soldiers had left the town, but there were still a few left who, together with numerous sympathizers, continued to fire upon the Americans from ambush, house tops, and particularly from the military academy. To quiet the fire from this latter place, it was necessary for the Chester and San Francisco to use their 3 and 5 inch guns, which they did with telling effect.

Additional troops were landed the second day, and the occupation of the city continued. By the third day the entire metropolis and its environs were in the hands of the American Marines and sailors, and the city was fairly quiet, with only an occasional shot being fired. Still at a later date additional Marines were despatched from the United States, under the command of Colonel L.W.T. Waller, at which time the Marine detachments as well as the sailors from the fleet were returned to their ships, and the Marines left organized into the First, Second and Third Regiments, and the Artillery Battalion, the whole being designated First Brigade of Marines, with a strength of 84 officers and 2,321 men.

The Mexican civil officials of the city quit their offices as soon as the American force made its appearance, and refused to resume their duties. Consequently, it became necessary for Admiral Fletcher to appoint Marine and Naval officers to these offices in order to reestablish a regular civil government for the town. By the 27th of April conditions were tranquil; shops and stores were opened for regular business and, from outward appearances, it was difficult to believe that the city was in the hands of an occupying force from a foreign country.

On the 1st of May General Frederick Funston, U.S. Army, with several army units, took over the command of all land operations and the Navy withdrew. The Marine brigade was detached from naval jurisdiction, reported to General Funston, and remained on such duty until the city was evacuated, on November 23rd, when they returned to the United States, and to naval control.

(Mexico)

During this operation the Marines suffered casualties of 3 killed in action, 11 wounded in action, and 1 accidentally wounded. The Navy's loss was 16 killed in action and about 58 wounded.

References: Sec. Navy An. Rep., 1870, 142-149; id. 1914, 49-52 470-471; Log of <u>Mohican</u> and <u>Buffalo</u>; Marine Corps Archives; St. Dept. Archives.

NAVASSA ISLAND

(1891)

For several years prior to the present one, an American concern, the Navassa Phosphate Company, had been engaged in gathering guano from the island, and had experienced considerable difficulty with their employees, who were negro laborers. This condition continued in varying degrees, until the early spring of this year when it grew worse, and the lives of Americans became endangered.

The *Kearsarge*, under the command of Commander Horace Elmer, U.S.N., was in the vicinity, and the Commander decided that the conditions warranted prompt action on his part. The quickest means at his disposal for the protection of American interests, was the Marine Guard of his vessel, which was under the command of an experienced officer of that corps, First Lieutenant George T. Bates.

On June 2nd Lieutenant Bates was ordered to take his Guard ashore and protect American citizens, their property, and other interests of his government in general. This duty was continued until June 20th, when conditions became settled and the Marines returned to their vessel.

References: Moore's Int. Law Dig., vol. I, 577; Sec. Navy An. Rep., 1891, 617; Log of *Kearsarge*; Marine Corps Archives.

NICARAGUA

(1852)

Early in the 16th Century Gil Gonzalez de Avila first explored the Pacific Coast of what is now the Republic of Nicaragua. His pilot, Alonzo Nino, discovered Fonseca Bay. Pedrarias Davila was the first governor of the province, and under his auspices the cities of Granada and Leon were founded in 1524. Throughout the Spanish era Nicaragua was a part of the Captaincy General of Guatemala. At the end of the Spanish regime in 1821, Nicaragua was successively a part of Iturbide's Mexican empire and a member of the United Provinces of Central America.

A constituent assembly at Managua declared an independent sovereignty on April 30, 1838, but intense political rivalry early became a major factor in its political history. Corruption attended the traffic across the country, along the San Juan River route, during the gold rush days of California, which added to the political demoralization, and the country has known little respite from internal and external trouble since 1823. The Republic of Nicaragua has not progressed as rapidly as other Central American republics, chiefly because of the frequent revolutions which prevented development of useful industries.

The first landing in what is now the Republic of Nicaragua by United States Marines was that of a funeral party from the Saranac, which landed on the 8th of January, 1852, at San Juan del Sur, to bury a comrade, Corporal Emory M. Vandever. A little later in the year, Commander Charles T. Platt, in the Albany, arrived at San Juan del Sur, and shortly after midnight of the 5th of February, a serious fire was discovered on shore. Commander Platt decided to send a landing party ashore to assist in fighting the conflagration, and detailed Lieutenant Armstrong, together with a detail of Marines and sailors, and the fire engine for the purpose. The fire having been extinguished, the party returned aboard about 5 a.m.

(1853)

Political disturbances around San Juan del Sur during this year necessitated the landing of Marines for the protection of American lives and interests. Commander George N. Hollins, in the sloop Cyane, was at this place in the early part of March, and on the 11th, landed his Marine Guard under Orderly Sergeant James E. Thompson for the protection of the American Steamship Company's property and that of the Nicaraguan Transportation Company; also American property at Punta Arenas where the Accessory Transit Company was located. They remained on this duty until the 13th, when withdrawn.

(Nicaragua)

(1854)

In the latter part of the preceding year, the American Minister to Nicaragua, Mr. Borland, while in San Juan del Sur (Greytown), was assaulted, and virtually kept a prisoner all night, being prevented from returning to the ship from which he had landed, which was then in the harbor. Commander Hollins, who had not been at San Juan since March, 1853, was directed to return to that place in the Cyane, and demand reparations for the indignity to the Minister, as well as for damage done to the property of the Accessory Transit Company, at Punta Arenas. He arrived there on the 9th of July, and forthwith demanded an apology of the de facto government authorities for the assault on the American Minister, and indemnity for the property damage. To this demand, the authorities made no reply. The Commander then issued a public proclamation that unless his demand was met, he would land his Marines and, if necessary, bombard the town.

Not having received a reply from the authorities by noon of the 12th, he detailed Lieutenants Fauntleroy and Pickering, the Marine Guard, under Orderly Sergeant James E. Thompson, and 15 sailors, and despatched them ashore to seize the arms and ammunition of the town. They captured three field pieces, several muskets, and destroyed a quantity of powder - returning to the Cyane late in the afternoon. Still there was no reply forthcoming from the de facto authorities. The doughty commander then prepared for the next step in exacting proper redress.

The following morning, the 13th, he directed the bombardment to commence. The starboard battery opened fire at 9, and continued, intermittently, until about 1:30 in the afternoon, when all firing from the ships' guns ceased - having fired in all, 177 shot and shell. At 3 o'clock the same afternoon, Commander Hollins despatched the same landing force which had landed on the 12th, ashore to destroy the town. At 7:30 in the evening they returned, having accomplished their mission. On the morning of the 15th he despatched a force, under Lieutenant Read, to Punta Arenas to destroy a quantity of powder. Now believing that condign punishment had been meted out to the Nicaraguans, the Commander sailed for other waters on the 17th.

Nicaragua's minister to the United States presented a demand for reparation for losses as a result of the bombardment of the Cyane, to which the Secretary of State, Mr. Marcy, replied: "If Nicaragua chooses to maintain the position you assume in your note to me, that her citizens who incorporated themselves with the community at San Juan

(Nicaragua)

are still in friendly relations with her and entitled to her protection, then she approves by an implication which she is not at liberty to deny [the acts] of that political establishment planted on her own soil and becomes responsible for the mischiefs it has done to American citizens. It would be a strange inconsistency for Nicaragua to regard the organization at San Juan as a hostile establishment on her territory, and at the same time claim the right to clothe with her nationality its members."

(1894)

The Tennessee adventurer, William Walker, was a spectacular figure in the Nicaraguan scene from about 1855 to the date of his death in 1860. After thirty years of Conservative control, during which the capital was permanently located at Managua, Jose Santos Zelaya, in 1893, began a sixteen years dictatorship. His regime was characterized by brazen speculations, and by mischievous intrigue in the political affairs of other Latin-American nations. The incidents surrounding the overthrow of Roberto Sacasa and the advent of Zelaya as President, caused the lives, as well as property of foreigners to be placed in jeopardy. The United States had two cruisers, the Columbia, under Captain George W. Sumner, and the Marblehead, under Commander Charles O'Neil, stationed in Nicaraguan waters to lend aid if and when necessary. About the middle of the year, the point of most danger appeared to be at Bluefields. Commander O'Neil put into this harbor on the 19th of June, and Captain Sumner followed on the 29th of July.

Shortly after midnight of July 6th, Commander O'Neil was awakened to receive important despatches from the American Consul, B. B. Seat, in which a landing force was requested for the protection of American interests. Orders were immediately issued for a detachment of Marines, under First Lieutenant Franklin J. Moses, and a company of bluejackets to be prepared for landing. Sometime between 4 and 8 o'clock, this force landed, under the command of Lieutenant Bowman, and remained ashore until the 7th of August. On the 31st of July, the force above mentioned, was reinforced by an additional landing party from the Marblehead, and the Marine Guard and a company of seamen from the Columbia, all under the command of Commander Charles O. Allibone, which were likewise withdrawn on the 7th of August.

(1896)

The first term of Zelaya as president expired in this year, but he forced his re-election, and continued his regime as virtual dictator. This caused a great deal of dissension

(Nicaragua)

— there being more than the unusual unrest among the people, and agitation between the different factions — which resulted in foreigners being again endangered. On this occasion the threatened area was that of Corinto.

The British government had a representative present in the person of the commander of H.M.S. *Cormus*, and the United States was represented by Commander Franklin Hanford, in the *Alert*. The Nicaraguan commandant requested the American Consul, Henry Palazio, to cause an American landing force to be sent ashore, as he was unable to furnish protection to foreigners with the forces at his disposal. The Consul communicated this request to Commander Hanford, who acquiesced by sending 15 Marines, under First Sergeant Frederick W. M. Poppe, and 19 sailors, all under the command of Lieutenant Albert W. Dodd. This force landed about 2 o'clock in the afternoon of May 2nd, and remained ashore until the morning of the 4th, when withdrawn. The British vessel also had a landing party ashore at this time.

(1898)

During this year the American Marines were again landed to protect the interests of the United States. Commander Eugene H. C. Leutze relieved Commander Hanford in command of the *Alert*, and arrived off San Juan del Sur in the early part of the year. In the first part of February the contending parties were engaged in open hostilities. Musketry firing was quite general, as well as artillery at intermittent intervals — some shells from the latter exploding in the water a short distance from the *Alert*. The American Consular Agent, Charles Holman, had acquainted Commander Leutze with the conditions ashore, and apparently had an understanding relative to the landing of Marines should their services be required.

About 4 o'clock in the afternoon of February 7th, the American Flag was hoisted over the Consulate, union down, and Commander Leutze immediately ordered 14 Marines and 19 bluejackets, under Lieutenant Harry A. Field, and despatched them ashore to protect the lives and property of Americans. Lieutenant Field and his landing party returned aboard about noon the following day, as the commander of the Nicaraguan Government forces stated he was then able to furnish adequate protection to all foreigners present.

(1899)

The Reyes Insurrection was the cause of disturbances in the first part of this year. The cause of the insurrectionists appeared hopeless, but the attending circumstances caused great excitement, and disorders were imminent.

(Nicaragua)

The United States was represented by Commander Frederick M. Symonds, in the Marietta. The British Government was also represented by H.M.S. Intrepid. These two vessels were at anchor at Bluefields, about the middle of February, when the foreign merchants of the city petitioned their commanding officers to despatch a landing party ashore to protect the lives and property of foreigners. The American Vice-Consul from Greytown, F. Percy Scott, was aboard the Marietta, and he together with Commander Symonds, went ashore on the morning of February 16, to obtain first-hand information relative to conditions. No landing was made, however, until late in the evening of the 24th, when Lieutenant Frederic B. Bassett, Jr., a detachment of Marines and sailors, numbering about 16 men, and a Colt's automatic gun, together with a like force from the British ship, were sent ashore to guard foreign interests. The American force returned to the Marietta about 7 o'clock on the evening of the 28th.

(1910)

A Conference was held in Washington in 1907, by which the Central American Republics agreed to avoid war and revolutionary disturbances. President Zelaya of Nicaragua, had consistently violated these conventions, and the Governments of Costa Rica, Salvador, and Guatemala protested to the United States against Zelaya's complete disregard of the general treaty and other agreements which had been signed.

To make matters still worse, Zelaya sanctioned the execution of two Americans in November, 1909. These Americans, Lee Roy Cannon and Leonard Groce, had served with the revolutionary forces under General Estrada, but were later captured by the Zelayaistas, summarily tried and executed. Upon Zelaya's acknowledgment of responsibility for this last crime against American citizens, Secretary of State Knox informed the Nicaraguan Charge d'Affaires that President Zelaya had notoriously kept Central America in turmoil since the Washington Convention of 1907, as opposed to the patient efforts of neighboring states to support the conventions. He further pointed out that under Zelaya's regime republican institutions had ceased to exist, except in name; that public opinion and the press had been throttled; and that any tendency to real patriotism had been rewarded by incarceration.

In the protests of a majority of the Central American Republics, to which had been added the protest, through revolution, of a great body of Nicaraguan people, and the illegal execution of the two Americans mentioned, coupled with threats against the American Consul at Managua, the Department of State found a sinister culmination of the Zelaya regime, and considered impracticable any further delay in

(Nicaragua)

active response to the appeals which had been made to it, and its duty towards its citizens, Central America, and civilization. The Nicaraguan Charge d'Affaires was handed his passport, whereupon President Zelaya attempted a reconciliation, but without success, and then resigned in favor of Dr. Jose Madriz. This maneuver failed, and Madriz then launched an offensive against the Conservatives and tried to recapture Bluefields.

In view of these conditions, several vessels of the Navy were despatched to Nicaraguan waters to protect American interests, and in the latter part of 1909 several Marine Corps units were likewise despatched, but no landings were made until early in this year. A regiment of Marines was embarked aboard the Buffalo, under the command of Colonel James E. Mahoney, and on the 22nd of February the vessel was at anchor at Corinto, when Commander Guy N. Brown ordered Captain John A. Hughes, with a detachment of Marines to proceed ashore to gain information. Captain Hughes landed about 8 o'clock in the evening, and returned aboard just before midnight, having completed his mission.

In the early part of April the Dubuque, under Commander Harold K. Hines, and the Paducah, under Commander W. W. Gilmer were looking after American interests at Bluefields, where General Larra was conducting operations. Both of these vessels sent a landing force ashore on the 19th of May, under Commander Hines. These two detachments not being considered sufficient to adequately protect American interests, the Dubuque sailed for Colon, Panama, on the 27th of May, to transport a force of Marines from that place. She arrived at Colon, embarked a force of 6 officers and 200 enlisted Marines, under the command of Major Smedley D. Butler, returned to Bluefields and, on the 30th, sent half of the battalion on board the Paducah. On the following day, Major Butler and the remainder of the battalion was landed in Bluefields, as was also those on the Paducah. On the 5th of June the bluejacket landing forces returned to their respective ships. Major Butler proceeded to Colon, Panama, on the 9th of August, secured the Marine band of 29 pieces, and returned with them to Bluefields. This battalion remained on shore at Bluefields until the 4th of September, when it was withdrawn and returned to Panama via the Tacoma.

(1912)

In the latter part of 1910, the American Minister to Panama, Mr. Dawson, was directed to proceed to Nicaragua to present the views of the United States to General Estrada. In October (1910), the Dawson agreements were signed. Elections were held in November; Estrada was elected, and

(Nicaragua)

assumed office on the 1st of January, 1911. The Zelaya party began to be a constant source of annoyance, and riots and vandalism were frequent throughout the Republic. The Chamorro faction within the Conservative Party sought to control the administration. This faction prevented Estrada from carrying through desirable reconstruction legislation, failed to cooperate in carrying out the Dawson agreements, and, on the 5th of April (1911), President Estrada dissolved the Assembly. The President then appealed to the United States for assistance, as in addition to his difficulties with the Conservative Chamorro faction, the Liberal leaders in the neighboring Republics were actively fomenting a revolution against his government. General Mena, Estrada's Minister of War, was arrested on the 9th of May 1911, by the President's orders. And on the same day Estrada resigned, turning over his office to the Vice President, Adolfo Diaz, who in turn released Mena. On the 31st of May (1911), as a result of a Liberal plot, Loma Fort in Managua was blown up, killing over 60 people, and two days later a magazine was exploded with additional casualties. A well defined revolution broke out on the 29th of July, 1912, and because of this unsettled state of affairs, the United States despatched several naval vessels to Nicaraguan waters for the protection of American lives and interests.

The _Annapolis_ was the first of these ships to reach the troubled area and, on the 4th of August landed a force of bluejackets (at the request of the President of Nicaragua) and they proceeded to Managua to protect American interests during the bombardment of that city by the revolutionists. The _Tacoma_, under Commander E. H. Durell, arrived on the 6th of August at Bluefields, and on the 17th landed 19 Marines and 38 sailors, under Lieutenant Bradford Barnette, where they remained until the 13th of October. A battalion of Marines, consisting of 13 officers and 341 men, under Major Smedley D. Butler, was hurried from Panama via the _Justin_, on the 10th of August. They arrived at Corinto on the 14th, and immediately landed. In the latter part of August, the _Denver_, and _California_ arrived off Corinto, and together with the _Annapolis_, which was already there, prepared to sending landing forces ashore. On the 27th, Second Lieutenant Earl C. Long, with 15 of his Marines, was landed to reconnoiter the railroad at Corinto and vicinity. He established a guard at Chinandega to protect the railroad, which was retained there until the 22nd of October, when withdrawn. On the evening of the 29th, a combined force from the ships above mentioned, consisting of Marines and sailors, entrained at Corinto for Managua. The _Denver_ then proceeded to San Juan del Sur, arrived there on the morning of the 30th, and landed a force of bluejackets to protect the American Consulate.

(Nicaragua)

The California sailed for Panama on the 28th of August to transport a force of Marines from that place to Corinto. She arrived there on the following day, and on the 1st of September embarked the 1st Provisional Regiment of Marines, consisting of 29 Marine officers, 4 naval officers, 744 Marines and 11 naval enlisted men, the whole under the command of Colonel Joseph H. Pendleton. This vessel returned to Corinto on the 4th and transferred the Marines to the Annapolis for further transfer ashore, where they landed the same day. The Colorado also landed her Marine detachment at Corinto, under First Lieutenant Lauren S. Willis, together with a detachment of sailors, on the 5th of September, where the Marines remained until the 11th of November. The Cleveland arrived at Corinto on September 14th, and the following day landed her Marine detachment, under Second Lieutenant Daniel M. Gardner, Jr., together with a company of seamen, 1 section of artillery and 2 Colt's automatic guns, the whole force under the command of Lieutenant Commander Edward Woods. This landing party remained ashore until the 23rd of October.

The greater part of the Panama battalion, under Major Butler, and the 1st Provisional Regiment, under Colonel Pendleton, was withdrawn on the 21st of November, leaving only a legation guard at Managua, under the command of Lieutenant Colonel Charles G. Long which consisted of 1 battalion of 400 officers and men. This battalion was relieved on the 9th of January, 1913, by a regular Legation Guard of about 105 officers and men, under the command of Captain Edward A. Greene.

During this occupation the Marines, unfortunately, had to resort to force of arms in order to dislodge a band of revolutionists from the Barranca, a fortified position consisting of two hills near Masaya, from which the revolutionists controlled and threatened the railroad and held the town of Masaya in a state of pitiable destitution. A short but gallant assault succeeded in overcoming the resistance. This engagement took place on the 4th of October, and as a result 4 men were killed and 5 wounded. In another engagement the same day at Chichigalpa, 5 other Marines were wounded, while on the 6th resistance was encountered in entering Leon, as a result of which, 3 were killed and 3 wounded.

Rear Admiral William H. H. Southerland commanded all of the operations on shore of both Marines and the navy personnel, as well as the operations of all naval vessels involved. General Mena surrendered to him, and shortly after General Zeledon died, and the revolutionary movement quickly ended.

(Nicaragua)

(1922)

During the latter part of the preceding year and the first part of this year, conditions became somewhat unsettled, and it was deemed advisable to increase the Legation Guard to enable it to handle the situation should circumstances so require. The Galveston, under Captain C. S. Kempff, and the Denver, under Captain A. Kautz, were at Corinto the latter part of January, when the Commandant 15th Naval District ordered that the Legation Guard be reinforced. First Lieutenant Edward E. Mann, commanding the Marines of the Galveston, together with 30 of his men were ordered to proceed to Managua on the 25th of January. On the 29th, this detachment was followed by First Lieutenant Arnold C. Larsen and 52 men. Additional Marines were despatched on the 8th of February. These consisted of Second Lieutenant William S. Fellers and 46 Marines, who had been transported to Corinto on the Nitro. Lieutenant Larsen and 13 of his men returned to the Denver, on the 11th of February, and the Galveston's Marines did likewise.

During the attempted revolt in May, the Legation Guard prevented the contemplated destruction of Managua, and through the good offices of the American officials, an amicable settlement of the difficulties was reached by the rival parties without bloodshed.

(1925)

Prior to this year the United States Government had informed the Nicaraguan Government of its intention to withdraw the Marines then stationed at Managua as a guard for the American Legation. President Martinez endeavored to have that policy changed, but was informed that owing to the notification of some fourteen months previously, in which time the Nicaraguan Government had ample opportunity to perfect plans, the policy would be carried out.

In November, 1924, Carlos Solorzano who was elected on a coalition ticket, to succeed President Martinez, was inaugurated on the 1st of January of this year. The United States formally recognized the Solorzano Government six days after Solorzano took office. The Constabulary, which had been provided for, had not as yet been organized, and President Solorzano requested that the Marines be not withdrawn until its organization, under American instructors, could be effected. This request was granted and the date of withdrawal was changed to the 1st of September, instead of that previously decided upon.

The Constabulary was finally organized, trained by three Americans (not Marines), and by the latter part of

(Nicaragua)

July, it was thought that the Constabulary had progressed to such an extent as to permit them to assume the duties of maintaining order, and allow the contemplated withdrawal of the Marines.

Instructions were accordingly issued to Major Ralph S. Keyser, who was then commanding the Guard, to make preparations for abandoning the post on the 1st of August. These instructions were carried out as planned, and the Legation Guard left Managua on that date, and sailed from Corinto three days later.

It is quite apparent that there was some apprehension as to the advisability of the Marines' withdrawal, due to a lack of confidence in the ability of the Nicaraguan Government officials to maintain order, and furnish proper protection to foreigners and foreign interests. How well grounded were these fears will be clearly shown in subsequent incidents which occurred in the affairs of the Republic.

Within a short time after the withdrawal of the Marines, various Liberal leaders, including the Minister of Finance, were arrested - it being alleged that these persons were implicated in a revolt against the Government. Disturbances increased, martial law was declared, and the railway was temporarily suspended through revolutionary activity.

On the 25th of October, supporters of General Chamorro seized the Loma Fort in Managua and announced their purpose of driving from the Cabinet the Liberal Members, and the restoring of the Conservatives. The pact entered into by the political parties whereby the Solorzano-Sacasa government had come into being was immediately broken, and Solorzano signed instead a pact with Chamorro, by which the latter was appointed General in Chief of the Army and his supporters placed in the Cabinet. In the following month, November, Vice President Sacasa fled from the Republic - stating that he was compelled to do so because of threats against his life. In December, the Nicaraguan Congress ordered Sacasa to appear to answer charges of conspiracy, but he did not return to Nicaragua.

(1926)

General Chamorro, continuing his climb to power, saw to it that his supporters in the Cabinet elected him to Congress, and, having gained a seat in that body, had himself elected first designate for the Presidency. On the 13th of January, the Congress impeached Vice President Sacasa and banished him for a period of two years. Four

(Nicaragua)

days later President Solorzano was granted an indefinite leave of absence by the Nicaraguan Congress, and General Chamorro assumed the executive power of the Government, even though he had been advised on several occasions by the United States Government that he would not be recognized if he assumed that office.

Notwithstanding this refusal, and the refusal of the Central American Governments, General Chamorro proceeded in his administration, apparently in the expectation that he could force recognition. Revolutionary activities broke out in May, which resulted in the necessity of again landing American Marines to protect the interests of the United States.

Captain John W. Wainwright, commanding the Cleveland, arrived at Bluefields on the 6th of May, and on the following day despatched his Marine detachment, under First Lieutenant Charles S. Finch, together with a detachment of seamen, on shore to look after their Country's interests. This landing party was commanded by Lieutenant Commander S.S. Lewis, and remained ashore until the 5th of June, when withdrawn. About two months later Captain Julius C. Townsend, in the Galveston, arrived at Bluefields, and, in accordance with orders of the Commander Special Service Squadron, despatched a landing force ashore consisting of the Marine detachment, under Captain Joseph W. Knighton, 6 naval officers and 132 bluejackets. This force landed on the afternoon of the 27th of August, and remained until the 1st of November. The Denver, under Captain Henry L. Wyman, arrived at Corinto on the 25th of September, and on the 10th of October sent her landing force ashore. This force consisted of the Marine detachment, under First Lieutenant Henry T. Nicholas, 5 naval officers and 63 bluejackets, the whole under command of Commander Selah M. La Bounty. They remained ashore until the 27th, when all were withdrawn except a Marine patrol of 12 men under Lieutenant Nicholas. Beginning with the 28th, this patrol was quartered aboard the Denver, but went ashore about 1 o'clock each afternoon, remaining until 6 in the evening, which practice was maintained until the 13th of November. Shortly after this the Denver sailed for Panama, but returned to Bluefields on the 27th, and on the 30th sent her landing force ashore there. This force was the same as that landed previously at Corinto, and the last day of this year found them still ashore.

In the meantime the Rochester, under command of Captain Burrell C. Allen, with a Marine company of 2 officers and 103 men, commanded by Captain John W. Thomason, anchored off Bluefields on the 2nd of September, and on the 11th, Lieutenant-Commander Clarence Gulbranson, Captain

(Nicaragua)

Thomason, and two squads of Marines boarded the steamer **Dictator**, which was lying in the harbor, and returned a few hours afterward. On the 13th they again boarded this steamer, remained a few hours then returned. A little later in the day this same party boarded the steamer **Camaguey**, remained aboard a short time, and returned. On the 31st of October, two detachments of the **Rochester's** Marines were landed - one in Bluefields proper, and the other at El Bluff. These detachments were commanded by Second Lieutenant Kenneth B. Chappell, and Captain Thomason, respectively. They were withdrawn on the 30th of November. The **Rochester** sailed for Rio Grande on December 23rd, arrived the same day, and immediately despatched a landing force of one battalion, including the Marines, for duty ashore, and they were still on this duty on the last day of the year On this same day (December 23) the **Rochester** sailed for Rio Grande and the **Cleveland** again landed her force of Marines and sailors at Bragman's Bluff, where they remained until the 4th of January, 1927.

It may be well here to give a very brief outline of the political set-up in the Nicaraguan Republic as they existed in the closing days of this year. A conference had been negotiated between the two political factions - Liberal and Conservative - which, after reaching an **impasse** state in the latter part of October, abruptly ended, and hostilities were again resumed. On the 11th of November, the Congress designated Adolfo Diaz for the Presidency, and the United States accorded recognition on the 17th of the same month. Two days prior to this recognition, Diaz through the American Charge d'Affaires sought the assistance of the United States to protect American and foreign lives and property. Doctor Sacasa (the former vice president) landed at Puerto Cabezas on the 1st of December and, surrounded by a small group of followers, was on the same day inaugurated by them as the "Constitutional President." He, in turn, named a cabinet, and became Commander-in-Chief of the revolutionary forces. General Chamorro, who had previously deposited the Executive power with Senator Uriza, resigned his office as General-in-Chief of the Army on December 8th, and on the 15th, he turned over the Army to the Diaz Government.

(1927)

The first of this year found the Marines from the **Cleveland**, **Denver** and **Rochester** still on Nicaraguan soil, where they had previously established several neutral zones for the protection of Americans and such other foreigners as might wish to avail themselves of the security afforded by the American forces.

(Nicaragua)

The revolutionary activities begun in the latter part of 1926, increased to such an extent that additional American forces were deemed necessary to furnish the proper protection to all foreigners, and to maintain the neutral zones. Accordingly, Captain Townsend, of the Galveston, was instructed to despatch ashore his landing force of Marines and bluejackets. This landing party went on shore the 6th of January, and proceeded to Managua, remaining there until the 1st of February. The Marine detachment of this force was again landed on the 19th of February, taking up a position at Outpost #1, at Leon, where they remained until the 15th of June, when withdrawn. At the beginning of January the Denver had Marine detachments at Pearl Cay Lagoon and at El Bluff, and they remained at these places until the 27th of May. On the 15th of July, Lieutenant Nicholas and 30 of his Marines landed at El Gallo, remaining there until August 8th, and on the same date First Lieutenant Charles Connette, with 19 Marines from the 51st Company, left for Puerto Cabezas via the Robert Smith. The Rochester's Marine landing force, now under command of Captain Franklin A. Hart, was withdrawn from shore duty on the 13th of June. The Cleveland's Marines, which were on shore at Bragman's Bluff, were withdrawn on the 4th of January, and on the 7th, 30 of them, under Lieutenant Finch, were again landed at Rio Grande. On the 9th, 22 other Marines were landed at Prinzapolca, under Lieutenant E.G. Hanson, U.S.N., both detachments remaining on this duty until the 6th of June. The Marine detachment of the Tulsa, under First Lieutenant John A. Tebbs, was landed at Bragman's Bluff, on the 17th of September, remaining until the 23rd, when they were relieved by Lieutenant Finch, with 27 Marines from the Cleveland. This latter detachment was in turn relieved on the 26th, by Lieutenant Connette with 25 Marines of the 51st Company, which was a part of the 5th Regiment.

While all of these landings were taking place, especially those during the month of January, the commander of the Special Service Squadron deemed that the ships' detachments were not of sufficient strength to care for the situation, and requested additional Marines from the United State. This request was answered by despatching the 2nd Battalion of the 5th Regiment, (under command of Lieutenant Colonel James J. Meade, which was at Guantanamo Bay), on the 7th of January via the Argonne. This Battalion landed at Bluefields three days later. The next unit to proceed to Nicaragua was Observation Squadron #1, together with 1 rifle company, under Major Ross E. Rowell, via the Altair and Melville, sailing on the 26th of February. The 2nd Brigade Headquarters, under Brigadier General Logan Feland, and the 5th Regiment, less its 2nd Battalion (previously sent) followed shortly thereafter, and landed at Corinto on the 7th of March.

(Nicaragua)

The opposing factions in the Republic reached an agreement on the 7th of May whereby the armed forces were to disarm. In view of this it was desired to have additional Marines to act as intermediaries in carrying out the pact. In pursuance of this plan, the 11th Regiment and Observation Squadron #4, the whole under Colonel Randolph C. Berkeley, was despatched to Corinto, the different units arriving between May 17th and 22nd. The Marine forces on shore in Nicaragua were gradually reduced, beginning about the middle of June, and by the last of September, consisted only of the 5th Regiment, less one battalion, together with one aviation squadron.

(1928-1933)

The withdrawal of the forces mentioned above, was apparently inopportune, because in the first part of this year it was necessary to reinforce the troops who were retained in the Republic, due to a renewal of bandit activities. The 11th Regiment, of 2 battalions, together with 1 squadron of aviation, were again despatched for Nicaragua early in January. General Logan Feland was also ordered to return to command the brigade. The different units of this last force arrived and disembarked between January 9th and 19th.

The outlaw leader, Sandino, began his active operations on the 16th of July, by attacking the garrison at Ocotal with about 500 of his men. This attack was apparently the signal for an increased activity on the part of the banditti throughout the mountainous part of the country, and it was necessary to distribute the units of the Brigade at all strategic points. These points were then held until the Guardia had been organized, trained, and property fitted to take them over and maintain them against opposition.

A number of the Marine officers attached to the Brigade together with worthy noncommissioned officers, were temporarily detached from their units, and detailed to duty with the Guardia Nacional as instructors and unit commanders - many remaining on this duty until a short time before the entire Marine force was withdrawn from Nicaraguan soil, January 3, 1933.

References: Sec. Navy An. Rep., 1853, 297; id., 1910, 20-21, 803-804; id., 1912, 12-13, 582; id., 1913, 534; id., 1922, 5; id., 1925, 59; id., 1927, 7-8; Major-General Commandant An. Rep., 1927, 8-9; id., 1928, 14-17; For. Rel. of US, 1907, 665; id., 1909, 446-452; id., 1911, 625-652; Logs of Saranac, Albany, Portsmouth, Cyane, Marblehead, Columbia, Alert, Marietta, Buffalo, Dubuque, Paducah, Annapolis, Tacoma, Denver, California, Colorado, Cleveland, Galveston, Rochester and Tulsa.

PANAMA

(1903)

The present Republic of Panama was part of the original viceroyalty of New Granada created in 1718, and about a year later beOame a part of the independent nation of Colombia. In 1841 Panama and Veragua provinces seceded as the state of the Isthmus of Panama. The constitution of the Grenadine Confederation of 1853 gave the states the right to withdraw, and in 1857 Panama seceded again, but soon returned. In 188. a constitution was drawn which denied Panama sovereign right; and made it a department, instead of a state of Colombia.

A treaty was entered into between the United States and New Granada, in 1846, which granted transportation facilities etc., to the American government across the Isthmus, and in turn the United States guaranteed the sovereignty of New Granada. This had been considered the first step toward the establishment of an American protectorate over the Isthmus. Another treaty, the Hay-Pauncefote, was negotiated and ratified by the United States Senate, December 16, 1901, which gave the United States alone the right to build and control an interoceanic canal across the Isthmus of Panama. In January 1903, still another treaty was negotiated, but it was not ratified by the Colombian Congress, possibly because it was hoped that settlement might be delayed until the concession of the company expired, and that then the payment from the United States would come directly to the Colombian government. The Congress, which had been specially called to ratify this treaty, adjourned on October 30th, and four days later Panama declared her independence. The uprising incident to this declaration occurred at 6:00 p.m. November 3rd, and the overthrow was accomplished without bloodshed. The organization of a new government was immediately started which was virtually recognized by the United States on the 6th

Rumors of an intended revolution had persisted for some time prior to its actual occurrence, and the United States government had despatched several naval vessels to that locality to observe and report on conditions. The commanders of these vessels had received special instructions as to their actions and duties, upon reaching the Isthmus, should an uprising occur or be in progress at the time.

The gunboat <u>Nashville</u>, under the command of Commander John Hubbard, was the first of these vessels to arrive in the area. She arrived at Colon and came to anchor at 5:30 p.m. November 2nd. Shortly before midnight the <u>Cartagena</u>, a Colombian troop ship came in and anchored near the <u>Nashville</u>, and about 8:00 a.m. the 3rd, she disembarked her troops, which numbered 500, including the general commanding The destination of these troops was reported to be Panama

(Panama) 135

City, but it was desirable that they not be permitted to proceed there, and the general commanding them was finally persuaded to that effect.

While these Colombian troops remained on shore almost anything could have happened. Quite a number of American citizens where in the city, an American consulate was located there, and it was a terminus for the American owned Panama railroad. As Commander Hubbard's instructions were to protect all American interests, he landed the Marines from the Nashville shortly after noon of the 4th, under the command of Lieutenant-Commander H.M. Witzel, and they took up a position in the railroad office. This landing party returned aboard at about 7:00 p.m., but were landed again the following morning, the 5th.

On the evening of the 5th, the Dixie, under the command of Commander Francis H. Delano, the second American ship to arrive at Colon, came in and anchored in the harbor. Shortly after her arrival, the Colombian troops sailed from Colon on the Royal Mail steamer Orinoco. Commander Hubbard and Commander Delano conferred together relative to conditions o shore and as to future action to be taken on their part, and decided that a larger landing force was required for the protection of American interests. Accordingly, two companies of Marines, under command of Major John A. Lejeune, were landed about 7:55 p.m. of the 5th, relieving those from the Nashville, who returned to their ship. The latter force returned to their ship shortly after noon, the 6th.

At 8:35 p.m. the 6th, the Nashville left Colon for Porto Bello, where she arrived the following day. The Dixie remained at Colon. On the 15th a small detachment of Marines were sent ashore, due to a slight disturbance on the Hamburg dock, but were withdrawn the following morning after a conference between the five Colombian commissioners, who had arrived earlier, and Rear Admiral Coghlan, on the Mayflower. However, the same evening (16th), Marines were again landed to act as a signal squad during the night, and continued this duty until the 8th of December. On this date Captain N.G. Burton and W. McCreary and Lieutenant F.A. Ramsey, U.S.M.C., and a part of Company B, Marine Battalion, on the Dixie, were landed and proceeded to Empire (about 30 miles from Colon on the Panama Railroad), for the purpose of establishing a camp. The same afternoon the remainder of the company was also landed, and on the 16th, the entire battalion under Major J.A. Lejeune, went into camp at Empire.

In the meantime other Marine organizations were being assembled at Philadelphia, Pa., and other places for service

(Panama)							136

in Panama. The *Prairie*, under command of Commander A.V. Wadhams, sailed from Guantanamo Bay, Cuba, for Colon, on December 11th, with a battalion of Marines under Major L.C. Lucas, to augment the force already there, and arrived on the 13th. The battalion was landed on the 24th, and went into camp. The *Dixie* left Colon on December 17th for Philadelphia, where she embarked a regiment, under Colonel L.W.T. Waller, and sailed for Colon on the 28th.

(1904)

The *Dixie* arrived at Colon the first part of January, and on the 7th landed both battalions - the First under James E. Mahoney, proceeding to Bas Obispo, and the Second under Major Eli K. Cole, to Empire, Panama. The battalion which landed from the *Prairie* on December 24th, was reembarked on February 15th, and returned to Guantanamo Bay, Cuba.

From the time of the first landing (November 4, 1903) until January 21, 1914, with the exceptions previously noted, United States Marines were stationed on the Isthmus of Panama to guard the interests of the American Government. On the latter date, all Marines were withdrawn.

References: Latane, U.S. & Latin America, 181,188-189; Logs of *Nashville*, *Prairie*, *Dixie* and *Atlanta*; Marine Corps Archives; St. Dept. Archives.

PERU

(1835)

From the date of the Peruvian Congress of 1822, to the administration of President Gamarra, internal disturbances had continued in this republic. Toward the close of his term of office, an incident occurred which finally brought about the revolution of February, 1835. The partisans of Orbegoso and Bermudez illegally nominated them as successors to Gamarra, which nearly brought the contending factions to a test of arms. A reconciliation of their differences took place on the eve of battle; and Orbegoso was elected to govern the affairs of State.

Prominent in this affair had been (General) Salaverry, a man anxious to gain control for himself, and his constituents. Therefore, he induced disturbances to distract attention from his activities, secretly organized a considerable army, ousted Orbegoso, proclaimed himself chief of Peru, and galloped into Lima as its master on February 25th. However, Orbegoso was not to be so easily deposed, as indicated by immediate resort to the use of the forces remaining loyal to him. The subsequent actions of these forces brought about deplorable conditions throughout the country, especially at Lima, the capital, and Callao, the chief port of entry.

On December 6th several American citizens petitioned the American Charge d'Affaires, Mr. Samuel Larned "to cause 40 to 50 Marines to be landed" for their protection, and the guarding of their property. The United States flagship Brandywine, under Captain David Deacon, with the Commander of the Pacific squadron, Captain Alexander S. Wadsworth, aboard, was in the harbor at Callao at the time. Just prior to the 10th of December, the Charge, believing the American Consulate to be in danger, requested Commodore Wadsworth to send a Marine guard for its protection. This request was complied with on the 10th, and Corporal Henry Bell, and Privates John Batham, Deodatur Nicklin and George Preston were sent to Lima for the purpose. Both factions having temporarily transferred their activities to other points, Lima was left without either military or civil government for several days, and conditions in the city became more chaotic.

The American Charge again having requested Marines, the Commodore on the 17th sent the remainder of the Marine Guard ashore under Captain Charles C. Tupper of the Marines. These Marines were quartered in different American houses, but the majority were at the Consulate. Captain Wadsworth, in his report says: " * * * there is no doubt but the presence of the Marines prevented a general plunder. As it was no foreign houses were plundered. The English and French Marines were sent up a few days after our own. * * *"

(Peru)

(1836)

The first of this year found the United States Marines of the Brandywine, still on duty in the capital city, Lima. All communications between this city and Callao had been severed, and a blockade of the port had been decreed. President Orbegoso then made Chorillos the port of entry, but Colonel Solar - one of Salaverry's men, who was commandant of Callao - notified Commodore Wadsworth that that port, too, had been declared in a state of blockade. The Commodore denied the Commandant's right to declare a blockade, informed him that American vessels would be protected against molestation for any infraction of it, and immediately sent the Boxer to that port to enforce his decision.

The Marines under Captain Tupper remained on duty at Lima until January 24th, when they were withdrawn, and returned to their ship. The Brandywine sailed from Callao on March 1st, but returned several times during the remainder of the year. One of these occasions was on August 31st, at which time Private Alexander Cady was sent to Lima for duty at the American Consulate. He remained until December 2nd, when he rejoined the ship at Callao.

From January 19th to 23rd, 1836, several people were given shelter on board the Brandywine because of the serious conditions in Callao.

References: Enock, Hist. Peru, 66-70; Log of Brandywine; Captains Letters, Jan. '36, #45, and Feb. '36 #32, Navy Archives; Marine Corps Archives.

PORTO RICO
(1824)

In the latter part of this year an American mercantile house in St. Thomas had been robbed, and there was satisfactory evidence that the goods stolen had been carried by pirates into Foxardo, a small port on the east end of Porto Rico, then a colonial possession of Spain. In the latter part of October Lieutenant C.T. Platt, of the U.S.S. Beagle was in this vicinity, and was informed of the robbery. He agreed to aid in recovering the stolen goods, and proceeded to the Port of Foxardo for that purpose. Arriving there on the 26th, he waited upon the proper civil officers, who treated him roughly, demanded his commission, which, when sent for, they pronounced a forgery, charged him with being a pirate, and finally arrested him and Lieutenant Ritchie, who had accompanied him, and detained them under guard during the day. After enduring various insults on the part of the officials and the inhabitants, they were permitted to return to their vessel.

Lieutenant Platt immediately set sail and, as he was running off the coast, met the John Adams standing in, with Commodore David Porter aboard. He went aboard her and reported the treatment he had received to the Commodore. The decision of the latter was soon formed; he deemed this an insult to the American Flag, which must be atoned for. The Commodore's ship could not enter the harbor at Foxardo because of shallow water, so she was anchored outside. Taking her boats and the Beagle and Grampus, he proceeded into the harbor, to carry out his plans. On the way into the harbor, and when the ships were about to anchor, it was perceived that a shore battery was preparing to fire upon the landing party. A boat was immediately sent with a detachment of 14 Marines, under Lieutenant Thomas B. Barton of the Marines, (a passenger on board the Grampus), to spike the guns; meeting no resistance from the Spaniards they quickly accomplished their mission and returned.

Commodore Porter landed with 200 Marines and sailors (officers and men), and addressed a letter to the Alcalde, dated November 12th, reciting the facts of the injury, demanding explanation and atonement, threatening to make the town responsible in case of refusal, and despatched it by Lieutenant Stribling under a flag of truce. One hour was given for a reply. Lieutenant H.N. Crabb, with 27 of his Marines was ordered to place himself in advance of the column and escort the flag of truce to the town. When within a short distance of the town the Marines halted to await the return of Lieutenant Stribling. A short time afterward he returned, in company with the Governor and Captain of the Port, who humbly apologized for the wrong they had done and promised thereafter to respect the rights

(Porto Rico) 140

of American officers. This apology was accepted, and after marching through the town the party returned to their vessels.

Commodore Porter's report of this affair called forth an order, dated December 27th, for his return home. The United States Government deemed that he had overstepped his authority. He was subsequently tried by a general court-martial, at the Marine Barracks in Washington, and convicted on August 10, 1825. With the sentence of six month's suspension was coupled a tribute to his zeal for the naval service, but Porter promptly resigned. A little later he was engaged by Mexico, as "General of Marine," to reorganize and command her naval forces as commander-in-chief. He remained in that duty until 1829, when he left the Mexican service and returned to his home in Maryland, where he arrived in the month of October.

Andrew Jackson, having become President of the United States, offered to reinstate Commodore Porter in his old position in the Navy, but Porter declined. Failing in this, Jackson appointed him Consul General to Algiers on March 18, 1830, which position he held until appointed Charge d'Affaires in Turkey April 15, 1831. He became Minister Resident on March 3, 1839 and died exactly four years later.

References: McClellan's Hist. U.S. Marine Corps; Memo Solic. St. Dept., 49-50; Nav. Inst. Proc., Dec. 1911, 1235-1238; Cooper, Hist. Navy, III, 29; Log of John Adams; Marine Corps Archives; St. Dept. Archives; Address, Con. Gen. Ravndal, July 4, '22.

RUSSIA

(1905)

In this year the first landing by American Marines took place on Russian soil. Honorable George von L. Meyer, American Ambassador at St. Petersburg, was appointed in March of this year, and a short time after taking over his new duties, apparently desired a small Marine Guard for the Embassy. The Brigadier General, Commandant of the Marine Corps, George F. Elliott, was consulted in the matter, and informed the Secretary of the Navy that such a guard could be furnished whenever so ordered.

A few days later the Secretary directed the Commandant to select two trustworthy Marines, and order them to proceed to Paris, France, where upon arrival they were to report to Commander Roy C. Smith, U.S. Navy, Naval Attache, United States Embassy, for such duty as might be assigned.

Quartermaster Sergeant Edward H.W. Holt, and Gunnery Sergeant Edward F. Larkin, were selected for this important duty, and sailed from the port of New York on the Kronprinz Wilhelm on the 21st of November. Later they proceeded to St. Petersburg, reported to Mr. Meyer, and remained on this duty until the 1st of January, 1907, when they were relieved and returned to the United States.

(1918)

The overthrow of the Czarist government by the Bolsheviki, was the occasion for great excitement, rioting, pillaging and murder, which soon spread to all parts of the Russian Empire. Vladivostok, even though many thousands of miles from White Russia, soon felt the effects of the Bolsheviki movement, and it, too, was soon in turmoil

Early in this year Rear Admiral Austin M. Knight in the Brooklyn arrived at Vladivostok to look after the interests of the United States. A number of other foreign powers also had vessels and troops at this place. The Czech and Bolsheviki troops were almost constantly engaged in active hostilities which endangered foreign lives.

These activities grew more serious from day to day and on the 29th of June the Czecho-Slovak troops moved in to occupy the city and its suburbs. They disarmed and imprisoned the Red Guard, arrested Germans and Austrians, and assumed complete control of the city pending the formation of a responsible government. About 5 o'clock in the evening Admiral Knight despatched Second Lieutenant Conrad S. Grove and 31 of the Marines on shore to guard the American Consulate. Two hours later Captain Archie F. Howard proceeded ashore to relieve Lieutenant Grove. English marines

(Russia)

were landed from H.M.S. Suffolk, and the Chinese landed a force from the cruiser Hai-Yung.

This state of affairs continued until the 6th of July. On this date Admiral Knight's chief of staff, together with representatives of the other powers present, called officially on the mayor of Vladivostok and delivered the following proclamation: "In view of the dangers which threaten Vladivostok and the Allied Forces here assembled from the open and secret activities of Austro-German war prisoners, spies and emissaries, the City and its vicinity are hereby taken under the temporary protection of the Allied Powers and all necessary measures will be taken for its defense against dangers both external and internal. All orders heretofore issued by the Czecho-Slovak authorities continue in force. The authority of the Zemstov and Municipality will be recognized in local affairs but the local military force and policies will be supplemented by such Allied Force as may be found necessary in emergency to prevent danger from Austro-German agencies and influence which are known to be at work in the city. This action is taken in a spirit of sympathetic friendship for the Russian people without reference to any political faction or party and in the hope that the period of tranquility which will result may permit the reconciling of all factions and their cooperation in a harmonious and patriotic effort for the establishment of a stable and permanent government and for throwing off the yoke of tyrannical dictation which the Austro-German Powers are endeavoring to fasten permanently upon the Russian people. All good citizens are enjoined to cooperate in the maintenance of law and order." This proclamation was signed by Admiral Knight and representatives of Japan, England, France, China, and of the Czecho-Slovak Army.

The Consulate guard (established 29th June) was apparently continued until the 10th of August, as that is the last date on which it is mentioned in the log of the Brooklyn. From August 4th to 24th, a U.S. Marine Corps patrol was maintained at the Russian Navy Yard, commanded by one of the two Marine officers mentioned.

(1919)

The next landing by American Marines at this place was on the 30th of July of this year, at Tyutuke Bay, which is only a short distance from Vladivostok. Captain Edgar B. Larimer, in the New Orleans, arrived at this place on the morning of the above mentioned date and immediately sent a landing force ashore to protect American interests. First Lieutenant Leland S. Swindler commanded the 31 Marines which this vessel carried. This landing party returned aboard in the early afternoon of August 1st.

(Russia)

(1920)

The United States maintained a radio station on Russian Island (Bay of Vladivostok) and due to the unsatisfactory conditions in Vladivostok, deemed it advisable to establish a Marine guard to protect the station and property. On February 16th this guard was organized, consisting of First Sergeant Thomas J. Treadwell and 17 other Marines, and a like guard was maintained until November 19th, 1922.

(1934)

The Government of the United States had recognized the Soviet Republic at 11:45 p.m. on the 16th of November of the previous year. The following day William C. Bullitt was selected to represent his country, as the first Ambassador to the Union of Soviet Socialist Republics. He received a recess appointment on the 21st of November, presented his credentials on the 13th of December, and was confirmed on the 11th of January of the present year.

After the recognition of the Soviet Republic, it was the desire of the United States State Department to have detailed five naval and Marine Corps officers as attaches to the Embassy at Moscow, but owing to a lack of funds for their maintenance only one was appointed. This appointment fell to the Marines, and Captain David R. Nimmer (then on detail in the Office of Naval Intelligence) was detailed as Assistant Naval Attache on the 29th of January, this year.

In addition to attaches, a suitable Marine Guard for the Embassy was also desired by the State Department, and on the 12th of February the Navy Department was requested to detail six Marines for such duty. The Marine Corps selected six noncommissioned officers and despatched them to Moscow on the 13th. They sailed from New York aboard the S.S. Washington, arrived at Hamburg, Germany, the 23rd, and there entrained for Moscow via Berlin, finally arriving at their destination on the 1st of March, where they are still on duty.

References: Case of Holt, E.H.W. #78312; Logs of Brooklyn and New Orleans; Marine Corps Archives; St. Dept. Archives; Navy Archives.

SAMOA

(1841)

Two years previous to this time the Wilkes Exploring Expedition, headed by Commander Charles Wilkes, U.S. Navy, was surveying in the Southern Archipelago, and in October, 1839, his work brought him to the island of Samoa. American merchant vessels had been carrying on considerable trade with these natives for a number of years. The commerce had increased to such an extent that the United States established a commercial agency on the island in 1820, to look after American interests. Wilkes saw the possibility of increasing this trade, and also the necessity for rules and regulations governing both natives and foreigners in this intercourse. He deemed it essential too, that his government should be represented by an official with greater authority than that of a commercial agent.

Realizing these facts to be of paramount importance, he immediately set about negotiating a sort of treaty with the principal chiefs of the Island. A conference which had been arranged with the seven chiefs revealed their willingness to enter into written agreements for the future guidance of both parties. The British Consul, W.C. Cunningham, was present during these negotiations, and expressed his approval of promulgating a set of regulations which would bind all parties to certain modes of conduct in future relations. Commander Wilkes then prepared written "commercial regulations" embracing 16 articles which, in general, provided for: Protection for all foreign consuls - All foreign vessels to be received in ports of the Island - Full protection for ships wrecked on the shores - Natives guilty of murder to be given up - Payment of port charges - Work on the Sabbath prohibited - Trading in or landing of liquor forbidden - Apprehension of deserters - Permission to be obtained before landing passengers - Sick left on shore to be cared for by consul - Arrest of seamen after 9 o'clock at night - Fines to be paid in specie - Magistrates and chiefs to enforce these rules - Chiefs to elect one of their number as magistrate - And, that the regulations be printed, promulgated, and a copy furnished to masters of all visiting vessels.

These regulations were approved and signed on November 5, 1839, by Commander Wilkes, John C. Williams, W.C. Cunningham, and the seven chiefs, Malietoa, Jamalanji, Matclan, Peea, Tooa, Moli and Saga. The day prior to this Commander Wilkes "appointed John C. Williams Consul of the United States of North America for the Samoa or Navigator Group of islands until the pleasure of the United States is known. * * *" Mr. Williams formally accepted the appointment on November 5th, and signed the regulations as "U.S. Consul."

(Samoa)

Approximately a year after Commander Wilkes negotiated the "Commercial Regulations" with the chiefs of Samoa, an American seaman was murdered by the natives of the town of Saulafata, Island of Upolu. An effort was made to have the person responsible for the crime given up to American authority (as provided for by the Regulations previously mentioned.) These efforts, however, were of no avail, and other methods were necessary to exact compliance with the provisions of the treaty. Lieutenant William L. Hudson, of the sloop Peacock, was ordered to proceed to that Island, and obtain redress for the murder committed.

The Peacock, accompanied by the schooner Flying-Fish, arrived at Upolu Island on the 24th of February, 1841. Lieutenant Hudson made a peremptory demand for the murderer, which was answered by a positive refusal from the principal chief. Resort to the landing of a party of Marines and sailors was the only alternative, and, at daylight the following morning, the Lieutenant made all preparations necessary for such a landing. He selected "70 odd men," divided them into three divisions under Lieutenants (William M.) Walker and (Edward J.) De Haven; (George F.) Emmos and Passed Midshipman (Alonzo B.) Davis; (Roger) Perry and Passed Midshipman Hawson (?), respectively. In the meantime the sloop was Kedged to bring her broadside to bear on the town, and the "long guns" made ready to fire. The landing party was ordered into the boats, and instructed to take up a position on the starboard quarter while the ship fired on the town.

When all was in readiness, orders were given to open fire on the village with round shot and grape. The grape fell short but the round shot took effect, and after the first gun was fired, nothing more could be seen of the natives who had previously collected on the beach. After some 18 shots had been fired, the landing party pulled to the beach, and landed without difficulty. Two of the divisions were assigned to the destruction of the huts (some 40 or 50), while the third was held in reserve at the boats. The natives were conspicuous because of their absence – they had decamped with all of their belongings – and the Americans captured the town without meeting resistance. The match was applied, and the village was soon in ashes. This completed, the party returned to the ship. Upon arriving there, however, they were held in the boats, "a taste of grog" was given each man, orders issued for them to destroy the other towns – Fusi and Sallesesi – and they again pulled away for the shore.

They landed this time midway between these two villages, one division proceeded to each and the third remaining with the boats, where they found conditions as in

(Samoa)

the first - totally deserted. There were upward of 100 huts in the two towns, and they were destroyed in a like manner as was the first. The mission having been completed, the entire party assembled on the beach, destroyed all of the canoes they could find and then returned to their ship, apparently satisfied that a well-deserved punishment had been promptly administered for the murder of an American seaman.

(1888)

That the punishment meted out to these natives, in 1841, had beneficial results, was evidenced by the fact that nearly five decades elapsed before the presence of another American landing force was necessary for the protection of Americans and American interests.

In September of this year a revolt took place against the Government of Tamasese. Mataafa was proclaimed king by the opposition, and a civil war ensued. In waging a warfare of this nature - especially between natives of cannibalistic tendencies - all foreigners resident on the Island were more or less in danger of losing their lives as well as their property. Even foreign consuls were apprehensive for the safety of their consulates, and their own lives as well. This strife between the natives reached such proportions by the month of November, that the American Consul General, Harold M. Sewell, requested Commander Dennis W. Mullan, U.S. Navy, of the Nipsic, which was then in the harbor of Apia, to land a suitable guard of Marines for the protection of American citizens, and the Consulate.

Commander Mullan immediately complied with this request by detailing First Lieutenant T. Glover Fillette and 10 of the enlisted Marines for the purpose, and sending them ashor on the 14th of November where they remained until March 20th of the following year, when they were withdrawn.

(1899)

A few days short of a decade had elapsed since the withdrawal of the Marine Guard from the American Consulate, before their presence was again required for the protection of American interests. This, as in the previous case, was occasioned by the outbreak of hostilities over the right of succession of the opposing chiefs - Mataafa and Malietoa.

The island had been recognized as a quasi-independency under the combined suzerainty of the United States and Great Britain, and the naval forces of both nations were actively drawn into the dispute, interfering to establish the claims

(Samoa)

of Malietoa as against those of Mataafa, and to put down the uprising against the former.

In February of this year Rear Admiral Albert Kautz, of the Pacific squadron, with his flagship Philadelphia, was ordered to Samoa to observe and report on conditions, and to take such action in case of emergency as he might deem warranted for the protection of American interests. He arrived at Apia on the 6th of March, and found that the British Government had also sent naval forces to the island, which consisted of H.M.S. Tauranga, Porpoise, Royalist, and the gunboat H.M.S. Falke. Captain Leslie C. Stuart, R.N., was the senior officer, and in command of the Tauranga. Admiral Kautz and Captain Stuart conferred relative to action to be taken in the case at hand, and apparently decided that a combined landing was necessary in order to settle the dispute between the two chiefs and their adherents.

A proclamation was issued by Admiral Kautz on March 12th, in which he adjured the several chiefs to repair to their respective homes and obey the laws of Samoa, and respect the Berlin Treaty of 1889, etc. On the 13th, conditions having become worse, a guard was despatched to the American Consulate for its protection and the protection of American nationals.

The following day the whole Marine guard, under First Lieutenant Constantine M. Perkins, together with a company of sailors under Lieutenant Field, a Colt's gun, and an artillery squad of 22 men under Lieutenant Brown, were landed at Mulinu Point "to remain indefinitely." On the 15th the natives began to gather in the woods back of Apia and back of Vailoa. The Philadelphia and H.M.S. Royalist opened fire on the former while H.M.S. Porpoise fired on the latter, with six-inch and 6-pounder shells for a period of about three hours. About 4 in the afternoon the American Consul, Mr. Osborne, his wife and son, went aboard the Philadelphia for safety, as did several other Americans and one Englishman.

Conditions grew even worse as the days passed and, on April 1st, it was decided to pursue the hostile natives into the interior, defeat or capture them, and bring the troubled conditions to an end. Accordingly, Captain Stuart selected Lieutenant Freeman, and British marines and sailors to the number of about 62, while Admiral Kautz selected Lieutenant Philip V. Lonsdale, two other naval officers, First Lieutenant Perkins, 20 Marines and about 36 sailors, and assembled the whole on shore for the expedition. In addition to these forces, the assistance of about 100 friendly Samoans was enlisted, and they accompanied the Americans and

(Samoa) 148

British in the attack. Lieutenant Freeman, R.N., being the senior, took charge of the column, and the march commenced along the shore in the following order: British marines, American Marines, the seamen next, then the natives, and the civilians bringing up the rear. The landing party, after passing the town of Faglii, cut inland, through a defile, and climbed to a higher plateau. They had proceeded along this for only a short distance when they were suddenly attacked in force from the left and left rear, by natives hidden in the grass. It appeared that the column was about to be cut off from the rear, and Lieutenant Perkins of the American Marines, ordered the left flank to fall back to a wire fence about 300 yards in the rear. By this time several men had been wounded, and were being assisted to the rear by Lieutenant Cave, R.N., and Dr. Lung, who agreed with Lieutenant Perkins that a retreat to the shore was the only alternative.

This course of action having been decided upon, a stand was made at the wire fence until the column could be assembled, the wounded evacuated, and the retreat begun when the opportunity afforded. Accordingly, four of the American Marines took position, and held the natives at bay while the command assembled. The retreat was now commenced, and the column finally reached the village of Faglii, where a signal was made to H.M.S. Royalist for reinforcements. After the landing force had arrested its retreat at Faglii, it was noted that Lieutenant Lonsdale and Ensign Monaghan of the American forces, and Lieutenant Freeman, R.N., were absent, and grave fear was entertained for their safety. This anxiety proved to be well founded, for on the following day the heads of the three officers were recovered from the place where the natives had beheaded them, and were buried with their bodies.

Besides Lieutenant Lonsdale and Ensign Monaghan, there were two sailors killed, and one Marine and four sailors wounded, as the casualties suffered by the Americans. Lieutenant Perkins, in his report of the affair, especially mentions three Marines as worthy of particular consideration: Sergeants Michael J. McNally and Bruno A. Forsterer, and Private Henry L. Hulbert. These three Marines were subsequently awarded the Congressional Medal of Honor for their conspicuous duty in upholding the traditions of their Corps.

A guard of Marines was maintained at the American Consulate until May 18th, when all forces were withdrawn and returned to their ship. On May 13th the Samoan Commission, which had arrived shortly before, was re-

(Samoa)

ceived aboard the flagship Philadelphia, with customary honors, and the conditions in Samoa were discussed. The bodies of Lieutenant Lonsdale and Ensign Monaghan were taken aboard the Philadelphia on the 20th, and sailed the next day enroute to the United States. She arrived at San Francisco on June 21st. On the 22nd and 23rd, respectively, the remains of Ensign Monaghan and Lieutenant Lonsdale were sent ashore accompanied by as many of the ship's company as could be spared, and a salute of three volleys was fired over the boats as they were about to shove off for shore.

References: Moore's Int. Law Dig., vol. I, 536-554; Wilkes Explo. Exped., vol. I, 1838-9, Let. #53; Sec. Navy An. Rep., 1899, 4, 922-923; Marine Corps Archives; Navy Archives; Logs of Peacock and Philadelphia.

S I A M

(1853)

As an illustration of the diversity of the duties performed by, and the reliance placed in the faithfulness and efficiency of the United States Marines, no better incident could be found for their portrayal than the recording of an affair which took place at Blenheim Reach, in the Canton River about sixty miles from Hong Kong, China.

On the night of September 11th, several naval vessels were lying at anchor in the roadstead, among which was the United States steam frigate *Mississippi*, with a Siamese man of war not far distant. Commander Sidney Smith Lee commanded the American ship, and was at the time asleep in his cabin. Shortly after midnight he was rudely awakened in consequence of the advent aboard his vessel of an overwrought foreign naval officer in the person of the Captain of the Siamese vessel, who stated that a serious mutiny had broken out aboard his ship, that he was unable to cope with the situation, and who begged the assistance of Captain Lee in regaining control of his crew.

Commander Lee, having had long experience in the naval service of his own country and possessing all of the characteristics and qualities attributed to the average American, readily understood from the manner and earnest representation the predicament in which the Siamese officer was placed. He agreed to lend succor in quelling the disturbance, but at the same time realized that the situation was fraught with dangerous possibilities. Whether the whole crew of the Siamese vessel or only a part of them had joined the mutineers, he did not know; the only information from which he could form an estimate being that from the commander, who was too excited to give a coherent description of the true state of affairs. Nevertheless, there was the spice of adventure dear to the heart of all Americans and, in addition, he had the faithful Marines to back him up in any undertaking he might elect to pursue.

Commander Lee, considering the possibilities involved, quickly came to a decision, ordered ten members of his Marine Guard to repair to the quarterdeck, a cutter to be made ready to embark in, and he, together with the still much excited Siamese officer, shoved off and proceeded to the vesse in distress. Arriving at his destination, he with the small party of Marines, boarded the ship of the mutinied crew, and in less than an hour regained control over the situation. Order had been brought about where chaos had reigned. His mission now having been completed, the doughty American officer returned to his own vessel, after an absence of less than fou hours, and was ready for any new eventuality that might aris

Reference: Log of the *Mississippi*.

SUMATRA
(1832)

This Island was the scene of many depredations by pirates for a number of years prior to the landing of Americans to avenge such outrages. Merchant vessels attempting to carry on commerce with the inhabitants were on numerous occasions plundered, burnt, set adrift, or otherwise disposed of as the fancy or interest of the natives indicated; the officers, crews and passengers were treated with indignity and violence, murdered, and, in some instances their bodies abused with disgusting barbarity. Conditions of this nature could not be tolerated indefinitely; the time had now come for the visitation of retribution.

The immediate cause of this retribution was the murder of the mate and two seamen of the American merchantman Friendship on February 7th, 1831, which was loading a cargo of pepper in the harbor of Quallah Battoo. Without warning, and without provocation the natives attacked the vessel, committed the outrage mentioned, and then plundered her of everything of value. Captain Endicott of the Friendship, with the assistance of several other merchantmen, was able to recover his vessel, but not until the savages had robbed her of about $12,000.00 worth of specie, and other property to a large amount. The voyage had to be abandoned, causing a loss to her owners of some $40,000.00, besides the unfortunate deaths of the mate and the two seamen.

Captain Endicott, with his vessel, finally reached his home port in America, reported all of the facts to his employers who, in turn represented them to the United States government, with the request that such action be taken as would prevent future occurrences of this kind, and to demand redress for the outrage perpetrated upon the crew of the Friendship and the vessel itself. The authorities readily agreeing to this request selected Commodore John Downes, in the frigate Potomac, as their representative, and instructed him accordingly. He sailed from New York on the 21st of August, 1831, touching at the Cape of Good Hope for information, and arrived off Sumatra on the 5th of February the following year. He disguised his ship as a merchantman, and then stood in and anchored about three miles from the town. Early in the afternoon of the 6th, the Commodore sent the whaleboat ashore with a party consisting of Lieutenant Irvine Shubrick, U.S.N., "the lieutenant of Marines" Alvin Edson, Lieutenants R.R. Pinkham, Henry K. Hoff and Jonathan Ingersoll, Acting Sailing-Master B.J. Totten, and Midshipman Henry Tooley, all dressed in sailor's costumes, to reconnoitre preparatory to his intended attack. This party returned aboard at 5:00 p.m., reporting that the natives had made a considerable display of armed men.

(Sumatra) 153

The C___dore ordered out all boats and had them made ready for an early attack upon the town. At 2:15 a.m. of the 7th, the landing party, consisting of the Marines and sailors, to the number of about 250, together with the division officers, the whole under the direct command of Lieutenant Shubrick, embarked in the boats, and proceeded towards their objective. This party reached the shore about 5:15, and immediately commenced the attack on the principal forts: Lieutenant Edson and his Marines in the advance. Lieutenant Shubrick had previously divided his force into three divisions - one of Marines, and two of sailors - and now directed one of the sailor divisions to take the first fort, while Lieutenant Edson attacked one in the rear of the town. The sailor division finally captured their fort after two hours of fierce fighting. The Marines stormed and took the second fort while the remainder of the force attacked another fort. This third fort proved to be a Tartar. The defenders fought with desperation, and it was not until the Marines and the other division of sailors arrived that the Malays were finally subdued and the position carried. The town was then fired and most of it reduced to ashes. The last fort was discovered when it opened fire, but was carried by assault and, by seven-thirty occupied and the American Flag hoisted over them all as a signal to the ship that they had been conquered. This victory had not been a bloodless one, however, for two had been killed (Benjamin T. Brown, a Marine and William P. Smith, a sailor), and 7 wounded, two of whom were Marines (Privates Daniel H. Cole and James G. Huston). Having destroyed all the forts, and leaving the town in flames, the landing party returned to the ship before 11:00 a.m., bringing with them those who had been killed, together with such wounded as had not previously been sent aboard. "At 11:30 (a.m.) committed the bodies of William P. Smith and Benjamin D. (T.) Brown to the deep with the usual funeral service."

Shortly before midnight of the 7th, the Commodore moved his vessel closer in towards shore - about one mile distant. At 12:20 p.m. the 8th, he opened fire, and bombarded the forts and town with his long guns and cannonades. This bombardment he continued for an hour, after which time a white flag was seen flying over the forts on shore, and the Commodore decided, before taking any further action, to give the natives a little more time for reflection.

The following morning, the 9th, a boat containing Lieutenant James P. Wilson, U.S.N., four other officers, and several Marines, was despatched to Pulo Kio, under a flag of truce, to reconnoitre, and investigate the conditions ashore. This party returned at 2:30 p.m. reporting that they had discovered white flags all along the shore line. After waiting

(Sumatra)

until 6:10 p.m. the Commodore's vigilance was rewarded by the apperance of a native boat putting off from shore, headed apparently for the American man of war. It soon came alongside, and it was ascertained that it contained a delegation of the principal chiefs, who expressed the greatest penitence for their misdeeds, sued most humbly for peace, begged especially that no more "big guns" be fired, and, finally, requested that all hostilities cease. The Commodore believing that they were sincere in their pleadings, readily acquiesced, but warned them that a repetition of these crimes against American citizens would be more severely dealt with than had the present one. His mission having been completed Commodore Downes weighed anchor, and the Potomac sailed from the Island of Sumatra for her regular station in the Pacific.

(1838)

The Chiefs of Quallah Battoo apparently soon forgot the visit paid to them by the Potomac, for less than five years had elapsed before a repetition of the same crimes made it necessary for another United States man of war to return to the Island, and bombard the town and forts as a punishment for such transgression. On this occasion it was the frigate Columbia, under Captaion George C. Read, and the sloop (corvette) John Adams, under Commander Thomas W. Wyman, that administered the punishment to the inhabitants, and the towns of Quallah Battoo and Muckie, or Mukki, for repeated offenses against Americans. These two vessels arrived off th coast December 21st and at 3:50 p.m. the next day, stood in and came to anchor off the town of Quallah Battoo. On the 24th they stood in closer to shore, anchoring about one mile distant. Captain Read then communicated with the authorities on shore, and made known his mission, together with demands for redress. He then waited until the 25th, Christmas Day, and not having received a satisfactory reply, decided to resort to other means to exact compliance with his wishes. About noon of this day, he ordered the commander of the John Adams to open fire. At 1:30 she complied with grape on some armed native boats in the river, and a few moments later with roun shot at the fort. She continued this bombardment until 3:00 p.m. when the Columbia signaled her to cease firing. The Columbia then continued the fire until 3:30 when she, too, ceased. The two ships remained idle until the forenoon of the 28th. At 10:00 a.m. the natives hoisted a white flag in token of surrender. A boat was sent in to communicate with the authorities and it returned thirty minutes later with the information that a chief would repair aboard the Columbi in a few minutes. Shortly before 11:00 a boat arrived, bearing one of the principal chiefs of the town. Commodore Read conferred with him for about thirty minutes and, apparently being satisfied, permitted him to return ashore. The follow-

(Sumatra)

ing evening, the 29th, the two vessels set sail for Muckie, the second town to be visited, but had proceeded only a few miles when they were forced to anchor because of a lull in the wind. Due to this delay it was not until 1:10 p.m. the 31st that they arrived and anchored in Muckie Roads.

(1839)

About the middle of the forenoon of January 1st, Commodore Read sent Lieutenant Turner ashore to confer with the authorities. However, the result of his mission was not satisfactory and it was decided to bombard the town. The Commodore waited, however, until the following forenoon, the 2nd - apparently giving the shore authorities twenty-four hours to reply to his demands. In the meantime both ships were hauled in closer to shore, and their broadsides brought to bear upon the town. No reply having been received the John Adams opened fire at about 9:30 a.m. She opened with round shot and grape on the forts and town. At 11:00 the guns of the Columbia joined those of the John Adams. Both vessels then kept up a brisk fire until about 11:30, when firing practically ceased, and the John Adams was ordered to send a landing party, under the command of Commander Wyman, ashore to destroy the forts and town. This party proceeded to the beach at 11:30, and landed without mishap, marched to the town and commenced its destruction. At 12:35 p.m. the Columbia sent a landing force ashore to join those under Commander Wyman, consisting of "the Musketeers, Pikemen, Marines and Pioneers." Both vessels kept up a slow fire on the forts until 1:05, when orders were given cease firing. At 1:45 the Columbia signaled to return aboard. The whole landing force returned to their respective ships at 2:30 p.m., having destroyed all of the forts, the town, and bringing two prisoners with them. The prisoners (native chiefs), were kept aboard the Columbia until early the following morning, when they were returned to shore. (Note: Lieutenant D.D.Baker, U.S.M.C., was apparently squadron Marine Officer).

The mission now having been accomplished, both ships weighed anchor on the morning of the 4th of January and stood out to sea.

References: Cooper, Hist. Navy, vol. III, 31-36; Vet. Bu. pamphlet of expeditions, 7; Logs of Potomac, Columbia and John Adams; Muster Rolls, Marine Corps Archives; Collum's Hist. USMC., 65-68; Navy Archives; Hamersly, General Register for 100 Years.

SYRIA

(1903)

Early in September of this year, Rear Admiral C.S. Cotton, U.S. Navy, commander-in-chief of the European Squadron, aboard his flagship Brooklyn, accompanied by the San Francisco, dropped anchor in the harbor of Beirut. About this time the Moslem and Christian people in this locality were experiencing difficulties to such an extent that an uprising was feared.

Admiral Cotton considered that the American Consulate might be in danger in the event of such an uprising, and took steps to protect it by making ready a landing force of the Marines and one company of sailors. This force was not needed, but a guard of Marines, and a few sailors, were furnished, at the request of the American consul, Mr. Gabriel Bie Ravndal, from the 7th to 12th of September, at which latter date they returned to their ship, the Brooklyn.

References: Log of Brooklyn; Muster Rolls, Marine Corps Archives; St. Dept. Archives.

T R I N I D A D
(British West Indies)
(1895)

The mission of the United States Navy and the Marine Corps is not confined to that of exacting redress from some island potentate, putting down rebellions in island republics, or fighting America's battles in time of actual war. Often they have served in bringing succor to some devastated country, relief to a city or town in times of serious conflagration, earthquake, or other catastrophe, when assistance was needed by suffering humanity.

Such an occasion arose when, on the 4th of March of this year, a serious fire broke out in the city of Port of Spain, Trinidad, which destroyed the whole of the business section, a large part of the residential area, and caused a property damage of about five million dollars. Nearly the whole populace were attending a cricket game outside of the city when the fire was discovered. The water service was defective, and the conflagration had gained such headway before it was discerned that little hope could be entertained for its control by local authorities.

Rear Admiral Richard W. Meade, U.S. Navy, with his squadron, consisting of the New York (flagship), Amphitrite, Cincinnati, Columbia, Minneapolis, Montgomery and Raleigh, was at anchor about seven miles off the city when, at about 4:25 in the afternoon, billows of smoke were observed rising from the direction of the center of the city. Soon after observing the smoke, flames appeared and it was easily seen that the conflagration was out of control, and that herculean efforts were necessary to prevent the city's total destruction.

The flagship signalled the Cincinnati and Raleigh, each to immediately select 50 picked men for duty ashore as a fire brigade. The flagship selected 25 Marines, under the command of Captain Benjamin R. Russell, and 100 sailors, and at 7:00 p.m. despatched them ashore under the direct command of Lieutenant Commander William Swift to assist the local authorities to bring the fire under control.

The Marines and sailors fought side by side with the local fire department for over four hours before the flames could be extinguished, and the Governor, Sir F. Napier Broome, addressed a letter of thanks to Admiral Meade for the assistance rendered by his force during this affair.

References: Sec.Navy An. Rep., 1895, XXIII; A & N Reg., March 23, 1895; Logs of New York, Cincinnati and Raleigh.

TRIPOLI
(1804)

Early in 1800 the Mediterranean "Pot", with its evil contents, began to boil. Treaties with the Barbary States and "presents" to them had kept the peace for many years. The system was vicious and voracious - they were never satisfied. At first we find that the only Americans who felt the sting of dishonor, were those who had to suffer the degradation of personally laying the tribute before the feet of the barbarians. The American navy and Marines long experienced this ignominy. Not only did they carry tribute, but they also suffered the insults and derision of the corsairs who neglected no opportunity of impressing them with the idea that they were "inferiors." It was upon these Americans that the odium of a base foreign policy rested, and it is to their undying credit that, notwithstanding all this and their abhorrence of such duty, they performed it with their accustomed efficiency.

Algiers, Morocco and Tunis were more or less complacent but not altogether satisfied, whereas Tripoli, feeling that she had made a bad bargain, indulged in threats against the Americans and remained adamant to all persuasive efforts on their part. The United States continued paying tribute at the point of a gun, which was completely at variance with the stirring battle cry of the Revolution: "Taxation without representation is tyranny!"

On the 14th of May, 1801, the Bashaw, to emphasize his dissatisfaction, ordered the flagstaff cut down in front of the American Consulate. Before the news of this act had reached America, President Jefferson had despatched a squadron of warships, under Commodore Dale, to the Mediteranean for its moral effect, but at the same time, it carried a "present" of ten thousand dollars for the Bashaw. This squadron remained on this station for several years. On October 31, 1803, the Philadelphia, one of the ships of the squadron, went on the rocks and her crew was captured, and carried into the harbor and imprisoned. Second Lieutenant William S. Osborne and 44 enlisted Marines were among the captives.

About the middle of February, 1804, Commodore Preble (who was then commanding the squadron), decided to destroy the Philadelphia, which was still impaled on the rocks before Tripoli. This was finally accomplished by Lieutenant Stephen Decatur and 70 volunteers, including 8 Marines. In August of the same year the Commodore bombarded Tripoli, but the release of the crew of the ill-fated Philadelphia could not be effected. Even the proffer of the sum of $100,000.00 as ransom proved of no avail. More ships were

(Tripoli)

sent to augment those under Preble, but the combined power of these, and the offer of still larger sums as ransom were insufficient to force, or tempt, the Bashaw to release the American prisoners. It required an "expeditionary force" on land to finally bring the Bashaw to terms.

During the summer of this year William Eaton, who had been "Navy agent for the several Barbary Regencies," conceived the idea of making a combined land and water attack on Tripoli, restoring Hamet Caramelli as Bashaw, and securing the release of the crew of the Philadelphia, together with a treaty foregoing payment of any further tribute. Commodore Barron was now in command of the squadron, and Eaton applied to him for a detachment of 100 Marines to lead his "coup de main" but was refused on the grounds that the Commodore did not believe his authority would permit such a step. However, Eaton was permitted passage on the Argus to Alexandria, from which place he intended to start his search for Hamet. He arrived at the latter place sometime in the latter part of November, 1804. On the 29th, Eaton, Lieutenant Presley N. O'Bannon of the Marines, Midshipman George Mann and 7 Marines landed and left for Cairo.

(1805)

Eaton and his party arrived at Cairo on January 8th. Here he learned that Hamet with a few Tripolitans had joined the Mamelukes at Miniet, where he was besieged. Eaton then pushed on to Fiaum, only to be stopped by the Turks who refused to permit him to proceed farther. Undaunted, however, by this setback, he found ways and means of communicating with Hamet, and made arrangements with him for his cooperation with the expedition against Derne, Tripoli. The next step in his plan was the gathering together of a force of sufficient strength to assure success of the venture, and to assemble them at some point from which he could make an early start. Eaton selected Arab's Tower, about 40 miles west of Alexandria, as his place of rendezvous, and here assembled a "motley" lot to the number of about 500. He also assembled 107 camels and a few asses to furnish the necessary transportation.

Having surmounted unnumbered difficulties Eaton and his party were finally ready to start the expedition proper, and on March 8 the long trek of nearly 600 miles to Derne was started by Eaton and his "conglomerate army." Many difficulties were experienced, such as dissatisfaction, mutinies and quibbling among leaders of the different factions, lack of rations, and many others. At one stage of the trip it was necessary to slaughter camels

(Tripoli)

for food. On the 15th they reached Bomba, and "the force was about to dissipate in disorder" when the Argus appeared with supplies. A few days later the Hornet arrived. Drawing on these two ships for supplies, Eaton procured the necessary food, etc., for his force, and resumed his march on the 25th. He arrived in front of Derne the same day. Under a "flag of truce," Eaton offered terms of amity to the Governor of Derne on condition of allegiance and fidelity to Hamet. The reply to this offer was "My head or yours." The Nautilus hove in sight this day, while the Argus and Hornet dropped anchor early the following day. Everything now being in readiness, the attack commenced "FROM THE LAND AND FROM THE SEA." Lieutenant O'Bannon with his Marines, a few Greeks, and such of the cannoniers as could be spared from the field piece, passed through a shower of musketry, took possession of one of the enemy's batteries, PLANTED THE AMERICAN FLAG UPON ITS RAMPARTS, AND TURNED ITS GUNS UPON THE ENEMY. After two hours of hand-to-hand fighting, the stronghold was occupied, and, for the first time in history THE FLAG OF THE UNITED STATES FLEW OVER A FORTRESS OF THE OLD WORLD where it had been planted by an American Marine - Lieutenant O'Bannon.

The Tripolitans counter-attacked the fortress several times, but the Americans would not give up the laurels so dearly won, and the enemy were repulsed each time with heavy losses. Finally, on the 28th of May, the Americans, by a spirited bayonet charge caused the retreat of the enemy from the vicinity of Tripoli. Memories of the Americans still linger in the songs of the women of Derne - "Din din Mohammed U Ryas Melekan mahandi", which means - Mohammed for Religion and the Americans for stubbornness.

This "Old World" fortress was held by the Americans until June 12. In the meantime, the American Consul General, Lear, had negotiated a treaty with the Bashaw, without mention of any "periodical tribute" but paying a sum of $60,000.00 as ransom for the American captives of the illfated Philadelphia. Indicating the confidence in which the Marines were held, they were given the honor of being the last troops (rear guard) to evacuate this foreign stronghold.

Before parting with Lieutenant O'Bannon, Hamet presented his "brave American" friend with the jeweled sword with a MAMELUKE hilt which he himself had carried while with the Mamelukes in Egypt. And so Hamet, through O'Bannon, gave to the Marine Corps THE SWORD CARRIED BY ITS OFFICERS TODAY.

Reference: McClellan's Hist. U.S. Marine Corps.

URUGUAY
(1855)

Revolution, and revolutionary intrigue, had held sway in the greater part of South America for a number of years prior to 1855. Argentina, one of the adjoining states, had been the scene of several uprisings during prior years, and it is quite possible that the unrest manifested by the inhabitants of that state had been communicated to those of Uruguay. Be that as it may, the fact is that about mid-summer of this year an uprising of revolutionary proportions spread over this country, and attained a character so sanguinary and disastrous that foreign residents were beseeching their diplomatic representatives for protection for themselves and for their property.

As had been the practice for a number of years, the United States had a squadron of her naval forces in South American Waters, whose duty it was to furnish protection to American citizens in cases of emergency. Brazil, France and Spain, also had vessels of war in this locality to look after their respective interests. These vessels and the American squadron were at anchor in the harbor of Montevideo. The United States was represented by Commander William F. Lynch, who commanded the sloop Germantown, and the American Consul Robert M. Hamilton. The commanders for the foreign vessels, together with the diplomatic representatives of their respective governments, held a conference and decided to make a combined landing of a portion of their forces for the protection of their nationals and consulates.

The landing previously agreed upon was effected on the 25th of November. The force was composed of the Marine Guard of the Germantown, under First Lieutenant Augustus S. Nicholson, and marines from the ships of the three other countries represented. After landing, they proceeded to place guards at the different consulates and the Custom-House. On the 27th, owing to the seriousness of the conflict being waged between the different factions ashore, additional forces were despatched to reinforce the Marine detachments that were landed two days previously. These additional forces, as well as the first detachments, were placed under the direct command of Lieutenant Nicholson. The reinforcements, however, were returned to their ships the same date, but the original detachments still remained on duty ashore. The American Marines were withdrawn on the 30th, after the revolutionists had capitulated, and conditions had become tranquil.

A short time before Lieutenant Nicholson and his Marines returned aboard their ship, an incident took place

(Uruguay)

which indicates the resourcefulness, bravery, and ability of the American Marine to act in emergencies. The insurgents had capitulated to the government. After they had been disarmed, the nationalists charged them, and a massacre would have ensued had not Lieutenant Nicholson and his Marines interposed themselves between the government troops and the insurgents to prevent such a catastrophe.

(1858)

Less than three years had passed when another revolution broke out in this small republic. No one faction seemed able to hold the reins of government for more than two or three consecutive years before it would be deposed, and another of revolutionary origin take its place. The lives of foreigners were jeopardized, and their property imperilled by this almost constant strife between the different factions who strove to control the administration of government.

Flag Officer French Forrest, flying his broad pennant from the St. Lawrence, with the Falmouth in company, was at Montevideo when conditions became so chaotic that he deemed a landing of Marines necessary for the protection of his countrymen and the American Consulate. England was also represented by a war vessel in the harbor. The American and English commanders conferred as to action to be taken, and agreed, as they had some two years previously, to combine their efforts in the form of a joint landing. Flag Officer Forrest was to command the combined force.

On the 2nd of January, in accordance with the prearranged plan, Forrest selected the entire Marine Guard of the St. Lawrence, under the command of Captain and Brevet Major John G. Reynolds, with 2nd Lieutenant William B. Stark as an assistant, and despatched them ashore. After the British had joined them on shore, the forces were combined, and distributed between the American and British Consulates and the Custom House. The American Marines remained on this duty until the 27th of the same month, at which time they were relieved by an increased force from the British ship, when they returned aboard the St. Lawrence.

(1868)

Little more than ten years of comparative tranquility was accorded the people of this revolutionary-ridden country before another outbreak occurred. On this occasion an armed force from the warships of six different

(Uruguay

foreign nations then present in the harbor of Montevideo were landed. These foreign vessels represented Brazil, France, Great Britain, Italy, Spain and the United States.

General Flores was governor, while his son Colonel Fortunio Flores, was in command of the Battalion de Libertad, which was the regular guard of the city. This Battalion had been turned against constituted authority, and was in armed revolt against the Governor. The Governor feared for his personal safety, and those who were loyal to him. Consequently, he applied to the American Consul, James D. Long, for protection for himself, his loyalists, and the custom house in the port.

This request was communicated to Rear Admiral Charles H. Davis, U.S. Navy, commanding the South Atlantic Squadron of the United States, who was then in the harbor with his flagship Guerriere, which was accompanied by the Quinnebaug, Shamokin, Kansas and Wasp. Admiral Davis received the Consul's letter on the 6th of February, and a little later in the day, also received a letter from the British Admiral relative to participation in a combined landing in the city. After considering the matter, he decided to cooperate with the foreign forces present, who, it seems, had received a like request from the Governor for the landing of armed forces.

The combined landing took place "at 5:50 a.m." of the 7th. The United States forces consisted of Second Lieutenant of Marines R.R. Neill, 15 of his Marines and 30 sailors, the whole under the command of Lieutenant-Commander Henry B. Rumsey of the Guerriere. When the various forces arrived on shore, they were placed under the direct command of Rear Admiral Amilcare Anguissola, who was in command of the Italian squadron then present in the harbor of Montevideo. This was done in consequence of his seniority.

These several forces remained ashore until shortly after noon of the following day, when upon receipt of a letter from the Governor, stating that the difficulties had ceased to exist, the foreign forces were returned to their respective ships.

This uprising had little or no political significance; it was devoid of any fixed purpose. Colonel Flores (the son), appointed no officials, made no attempt to exercise political authority, nor enforce police regulations. His conduct appeared to be that of a mutineer at the head of some three or four hundred armed soldiers who lawlessly throws into consernation and a state of siege a city of

(Uruguay)

70,000 inhabitants, two thirds of whom are actually foreigners, and leaving the sole reliance for security of lives and property to the aid of foreign men-of-war.

Admiral Davis in his report of this affair stated: "The predominance of foreign interests here (Montevideo), and in the large cities of the Argentine Republic, will probably render it expedient at no distant period, to confer upon them a permanent defence against these frequent insurrections or revolts, very few of which possess any color of a motive, such as would justify resistance of legal authority."

The Quinnebaug and Shamokin sailed a few days after this affair, and Admiral Davis followed them in the Guerriere on the 19th of February, leaving the Kansas and Wasp, with detailed instructions, to look after the interests of the United States during his absence. It appears that he had hardly cleared the harbor before a new outbreak occurred with disastrous results. Late in the afternoon of this date Governor Flores "was butchered in the street" by agents of the opposite party, and his friends rose in return and killed thirty or forty belonging to the party of the assassins. This incident, of course, threw the city into a state of chaos, and the assistance of the foreign warships was again requested to protect the custom house and resident foreigners.

Following Admiral Davis' instructions and in compliance with this later request, the commanding officers of the Kansas and Wasp landed 50 officers and men, who guarded the custom house, and the American Consulate from the evening of the 19th to the 27th. On the latter date they were withdrawn at the request of the President of the Republic.

References: Logs of Germantown, St. Lawrence, Guerriere and Quinnebaug; Collum's Hist. U.S.M.C., 105-106, 110-111; Sec. Navy An. Rep., 1868, XVI; St. Dept. Archives; Marine Corps Archives; So. Atl. Sqd. (Brazil), Rear Admiral C.H. Davis, June 1867, Sept. 1868, vol. I, letters #78, 92, 93, and 96, Navy Archives.

www.ingramcontent.com/pod-product-compliance
Lightning Source LLC
Chambersburg PA
CBHW080506110426
42742CB00017B/3011